AMERICA
IN THE
'40s

A Sentimental Journey

AMERICA
IN THE
★ '40s ★

With a foreword by
Bill Mauldin

Reader's Digest

THE READER'S DIGEST ASSOCIATION, INC.
Pleasantville, New York/Montreal

A Reader's Digest Book

Edited and Produced by The Reference Works
Editor in Chief: Harold Rabinowitz
Writer: John Klotzbach
Copy Editor: Diane Root
Design Director: Bob Antler, Antlerworks
Photo Researcher: Samantha Greene
Assistant Photo Researcher: Sarah Kramer

Library of Congress Cataloging in Publication Data

America in the '40s : a sentimental journey.
     p.   cm.
   Includes index.
   ISBN 0-7621-0010-9 (pbk) 0-7621-0081-8 (hc)
   1. United States—Social life and customs—1918-1945. 2. United
States—Social life and customs—1918-1945—Pictorial works.
3. United States—Social life and customs—1945-1970. 4. United
States—Social life and customs—1945-1970—Pictorial works.
5. World War, 1939–1945—United States. 6. World War, 1939-1945—
United States—Pictorial works.   I. Reader's Digest Association.
E169.A494   1998
973.9—dc21   97–40679

Acknowledgments
The editors would like to thank Richard Walker, Bob Gallagher, Alexander Hoyt, and John Klotzbach, as well as Debbie Goodsite of The Bettmann Archive and Peter Langdon of Corbis, for their contributions to this book. They would also like to thank Tom Spain Productions for conducting interviews on which the *Living Portraits* are based, and Andrew Fredericks, for providing images.

Picture Credits

Peter Campbell/Corbis:14; Corbis-Bettmann:12, 21-24, 25, 28, 29, 33,41-44, 49, 50, 52-53, 57, 60, 62, 63, 65, 66, 67, 69, 72, 75, 80, 88, 89, 91, 94, 96-98, 100, 104-107, 109-110, 117, 119, 120, 121-122, 124, 127, 130, 134-135, 139, 140, 141, 144-149, 151-155; Jack Fields/Corbis: 112; Franklin D. Roosevelt Library/ Corbis: 98-99; Angelo Hornak/Corbis: 15; Hulton-Deutsch/Corbis: 92, 105, 11; Library of Congress/Corbis: 22, 78, 99, 149; Kelly-Mooney/Corbis: 106; National Archives and Records Administration/Corbis: 46, 81, 91, 93, 99, 104-105, 118; Seattle Post-Intelligencer Collection, Museum of History and Industry/Corbis: 33; John Springer/Corbis-Bettmann: 28, 30, 34, 41, 44, 52, 92, 101, 121, 138, 149, 151; UPI/Corbis-Bettmann: 10-14, 15-27, 29, 30, 33-35, 38-44, 47-50, 52-53, 54-55, 58-59, 63-66, 68 -72, 74, 75-78, 81-84, 89, 90, 91, 93, 94, 97-99, 101-103, 104-107, 108, 113 -119, 122, 123, 124, 126-129, 130, 135-139, 141, 142, 143, 147, 150, 152-155

Cover montage celebrating the defining moments and personalities of America in the '40s reproduced courtesy of Corbis-Bettmann, UPI/Corbis-Bettmann, and National Archives and Records Administration/Corbis.

Printed in the United States of America

About this Book

The 1940s were a chaotic time for America: Born in the poverty of the Great Depression, the decade matured in the crucible of war and ended in prosperity and hope tempered by the anxiety of the nuclear age.

AMERICA IN THE '40S is a memory book of that turbulent age, an attempt to find the threads that connect the events and weave them into a coherent tapestry of the times.

The main threads of this book are the people of the Forties—the immigrants, sharecroppers, factory hands, businessmen, soldiers, sailors, musicians, miners, farmers, husbands, wives, and children. We have revealed them through the letters they wrote, the memories of their loved ones, and their recollections. And we have bound them together by their images and possessions—the arcade photos snapped hours before the troop ship sailed, the ration coupons, the movie posters in the Bijou lobby, the magazines on the newsstands, the newsreels, the advertising.

AMERICA IN THE '40S is the companion to the Reader's Digest video and PBS series of the same name. From the video, we have drawn the Living Portraits of men and women who tell about their own vivid experiences of the decade both in war and peace. From the Bettmann and Corbis archives we have selected more than 300 images of the decade, and with

the help of noted collector Bob Gallagher, we assembled five collages of objects that might have been found in a household drawer in the Forties.

Helping us get started

on the right foot is the cartoonist Bill Mauldin, who wrote the book's foreword and who, in the Forties, won a Pulitzer Prize for helping the nation understand war through the eyes of his characters Willie and Joe, two of the muddiest, tiredest, but clearest-eyed soldiers ever to hunker down in a foxhole.

Welcome to America in the Forties.

—the Editors

Foreword

By Bill Mauldin

In the late 1930s, life for me, and I would say for much of the country, was far removed from the events in Europe. We were just recovering from the Depression, happy to have enough food on our plates and a steady income to put it there. My generation had not really known how strenuous living with a war could be. Many of our parents had been soldiers. I had grown up hearing stories about military glory, the strength and fearlessness of my father's World War I battalion, and the glamour of being overseas—seducing beautiful French girls and the like.

We took it all with a grain of salt, but in fact it was my father's experiences during the First World War that inspired me to join the National Guard in 1940. I never heard my father speak of the brutality of battle or the unimaginable vulnerability of believing that your life might end at any moment. These must have been elements of my father's—and every soldier's—experience, because these elements of war were real.

Bill Mauldin is a two-time Pulitzer Prize-winning cartoonist whose work has appeared in numerous magazines and newspapers. During World War II he served as an infantryman in France, Germany, and Italy where he was wounded and received a Purple Heart. His army cartoons have been collected in Star Spangled Banter, Mud, Mules and Mountains, *and* Up Front. *His work is universally recognized as an American treasure.*

But he had survived that war and the struggles in the decades that followed, and he, like most Americans, had put the past behind him. Americans believed (or at least hoped) that everything was looking up, that we could breathe a sigh of relief because history had turned a corner. America was strong and stable. Finally, we could look into our future and see good times ahead.

Pearl Harbor awoke America from this slumber, momentarily shattering the almost-realized dream. The bombing changed American attitudes from invincibility to insecurity. In a matter of minutes, we went from one of the strongest nations in the world to a helpless giant of a country.

Suddenly, there was a genuine belief, at least in some quarters, that a Japanese battalion could land on the West Coast, and if they did, there was no doubt that they could go all the way to Washington with little opposition. From this moment on we were uncertain, vulnerable, afraid. We were confident that if we didn't do everything in our power to gear up the nation as a war machine we would be decimated.

Although I felt this fear, I did not really understand what war meant until I went to Europe. It was there that I saw men dying, that I experienced the helplessness of never knowing when you would be attacked, of needing to be doggedly alert, constantly. But you didn't have to be a soldier to feel vulnerable. For America as a whole, the best way to deal with this fear was by mobilization. Civil defense, victory gardens,

"This damm tree leaks."

munitions plants; the duty of Americans during the war was to rise above threats from abroad both to their own lives and to the lives of their loved ones overseas.

I think everyone, on the battlefield and on the home front, felt the weight of the war, but we couldn't both be solemn about it and continue on with our lives. So there was this balance in the American mentality—we had to keep a positive attitude despite the fact that we couldn't quite shake our fears or ignore the reality of war.

I was lucky because I had learned early in life to deal with hardship through humor. Military humor, in general, came from the implicit understanding that you might as well laugh at your situation, because if you didn't, you would certainly start to cry. This was the rationale behind my cartoons. Cartooning was my outlet. It was my way to laugh at, and comment on, the irony of a situation while still acknowledging that things were pretty horrible. Willie and Joe, for example, were not your strapping young bucks, arriving zealously at the front ready

to kill some enemies. They were what these strapping young bucks soon became—what we all became by the time we returned home. They were hardened, weathered, and weary, but they were not broken and their experience had taught them not to take everything quite so seriously.

Despite the struggles associated with World War II, wartime was also a period of growth, excitement, and energy in America. The war effort infused the country with a new vitality. People had a sense of purpose, virtually no one was left with nothing to do, and this feeling that they were necessary gave people a new confidence in their abilities. Sure, there was always worry about the war, but the country we soldiers returned home to was one that had continued moving forward while we were away.

More than anything else, the war had given everyone—soldiers and civilians alike—a chance to redefine themselves. Many types of people left the country to fight in Europe and the Pacific, but no matter who we were when we departed, we all came home as heroes. I will never forget my return from Europe, to be greeted by those crowds, cheering, waving. I remember looking behind me at the high-ranking

"Damm fine road, men!"

officers with whom I had returned and thinking that the fanfare was all for them, that they were the heroes and I was just a guy who did what he could, but I was wrong. Americans at home were cheering for me, and for every soldier who had risked his life to save others. It didn't matter who or what you had been before, you had killed the enemy, saved the country, and saved the world—and for that, America loved you.

The pride Americans felt in winning the war—that incredible sense of power and relief—gave us the ability to embrace the changes that war had ushered in. America was a new place after 1945. We had a new president, new cars, new houses, new neighborhoods, new clothes—our women were wearing pants—and opportunities that no one would have imagined a few years earlier. I was not only finally able to make a living doing what I loved, but later I acted in the movies. (Can you imagine a smart aleck from New Mexico on the big screen in Hollywood?)

For all of their tragedy, the 1940s were ultimately characterized by triumph. They were years of growth, when America gained a sense of her strength as a nation and Americans gained a sense of their strength as individuals. The 1940s shaped America as no decade had before in history, leaving a legacy that can still be felt in our world today.

These are the things I remember about the 1940s, and I was proud to be a part of the filming of AMERICA IN THE '40S and a part of the celebration of that era as it is presented in this book. I think many people turning the pages of this volume are going to have more than a few misty moments as images and words leap out at them from these pages.

No one is ever going to find a way to make war anything other than a horrible thing, something to be avoided if at all possible. But sometimes a period of war can be part of a nation's growing pains, and the Forties was definitely the decade in which America grew up. War set the wheels of America in motion thrusting us into the modern world with all its opportunities and all its anxieties. Life has certainly changed considerably since the 1940s, but this was the decade we took our first steps into adulthood and onto the road that would lead us to where we are today.

—Bill Mauldin

Contents

PART THREE 1946-1949
Changing Times: The Modern Era Begins 108

Evenings at home for most families meant gathering around the radio and listening to a favorite program. Above, a Provincetown, Massachusetts, family gathers to listen to one of President Roosevelt's fireside chats. Right, New Year's Eve revelers at the St. Moritz Hotel in New York City welcome the new decade with high hopes.

The 1940s changed America more rapidly than any other decade in history. In 10 years the country went from sleeping giant to superpower, from the simplicity of an agricultural-industrial age to the complexities of the atomic age, from a country whose army used rifles made in 1917 to the strongest nation the world had ever seen.

On New Year's Day 1940, as the new decade dawned, America was still a nation of small towns with white-steepled churches, of Main Streets lined with maple and sycamore trees, of general stores, picket fences, and front-porch swings. Just as small towns dominated the American landscape, so too small-town life defined the American character. In the 1940s the United States was still a land of box lunches at church socials, of company picnics and 4-H Clubs, of hand-cranked wall phones and party lines, of iceboxes, radios, clothespins, and pincushions, of seven o'clock breakfasts with griddle cakes, bacon, eggs, and coffee. Most women still sewed. Some women wore hair nets called snoods. Others used pads called hair rats to make their coiffure look thicker. Almost all of them made casseroles, pot roast, and pineapple upside-down cake. Children whizzed down neighborhood streets on roller skates and ate double-dip ice cream cones. A new DeSoto car cost $701 in 1940, and gas was 19 cents a gallon; but at the start of the decade most Americans did not own a car and couldn't even drive. Just 20 miles out of New York City, a common highway sight was a farmer in overalls driving a Model-T truck hauling eggs or chicken feed. In more rural areas drivers shared the road with livestock and mule-drawn wagons. Speed limits were much lower than they are today; road signs proclaimed: "This is God's country, so don't drive through it like hell."

The Look of the Future

As the country emerged from the Depression, most Americans were cautiously optimistic about the future. The

ROAD TO REALITY
America Prepares for War

Urban visionary Robert Moses had the knack of getting governments to fund most of his projects—but not all of them. Here he stands behind his model for an immense bridge connecting Brooklyn and lower Manhattan—one Moses project that was never built.

recession of 1938—though a recent and painful memory—already seemed, only two years later, to belong to a different era, that dark, anxious time of bread lines, soup kitchens, and Dust Bowl desperation. It was a time most Americans fervently believed was gone for good. There was a general feeling that the nation had at last turned the final corner to prosperity. Slowly, steadily, things were getting better.

Two World's Fairs, one on each coast, had opened in the summer of 1939. Both the San Francisco Golden Gate International Exposition and the New York World's Fair at Flushing Meadows were huge popular successes drawing millions of enthusiastic, curious visitors. The New York World's Fair was organized by master urban planner Robert Moses. Its theme was The World of Tomorrow. President Franklin D. Roosevelt formally opened the fair on the 150th anniversary of George Washington's presidential inaugural, becoming the first president to appear on television, his image broadcast over an experimental model.

In pavilions with names like Democracity and Futurama, fairgoers could see a model planned metropolis of the future or catch a glimpse of General Motors' idea of how the country's cities and highways would look in 1960—shiny, aerodynamic vehicles on clean, uncluttered roads, with nobody speeding or cutting anyone off. The fair depicted a better tomorrow, a brighter, cleaner world of peace and plenty, ease and economy, dominated by innovative technological marvels. There was a strong emphasis on bringing into the home the streamlining and efficiency that were quickly becoming the hallmarks of contemporary American indus-

Some construction projects soared high above the ground—Rockefeller Center (right). Others built deep underground—the Queens Midtown Tunnel (below).

trial design. The same sleek, silvery, modernistic, aerodynamic styling that was seen in luxury trains (the *Twentieth Century Limited*, the *Broadway Limited,* the *Zephyr*), luxury planes (Pan Am's *Clippers*), and luxury cars (the Cord, the Duesenberg) was reflected in affordable everyday objects like toasters, radios, irons, alarm clocks, coffeemakers and refrigerators. The fair also marked the first time fluorescent lighting and air conditioning were used on a grand scale.

Another cause for American optimism in 1940 was the completion of New York's Rockefeller Center. This magnificent commercial complex was the nation's most ambitious privately funded building project that had been started after the onset of the Great Depression. Principal designer Raymond Hood's plan called for a city within a city, a cluster of skyscrapers that would reflect the energy and power of modern Manhattan mercantilism. The centerpiece, the 70-story RCA Building, embodied the optimism of the day as it soared, slender but strong, cool and clean, into the sky of a bustling midtown. Despite the majesty, there was something warm and welcoming about the complex: the friendliness of the buff-colored limestone; the happy diversions of Art Deco ornamentation, murals, sculptures, and reliefs. It immediately became one of New York's most popular attractions.

A Time to Prepare

American industry at the start of 1940 was developing at a rapid pace. Early in the year Secretary of Commerce Harry L. Hopkins announced that the fourth quarter of 1939 had matched the best quarter of 1929. Two weeks into the new year, the Commerce Department reported that inventories, orders, and shipments were all showing gains. And midway through February, the United States Chamber of Commerce was predicting all-time highs for the month would be reached for virtually every industrial index. American industrial production, however, was clearly being driven by events in Europe that spring. For six months, the Phony War that followed the invasion of Poland made it possible for Americans to hope that the conflict

FDR assured Americans that war was not his first choice, even as he prepared the nation for conflict.

would remain a localized one. In March 1940 only two countries—Finland and the Soviet Union—were actually fighting. Though technically at war, British, French, and German troops had not yet exchanged a single shot, nor had they begun to drop bombs on one another. Then, on April 9, the Nazi invasion of Denmark and Norway shattered the illusion that the European war could be a limited one. On May 10, under Hitler's orders, the smashing German offensive against Holland, Belgium, and France began. Within the week, President Roosevelt had requested that Congress double its appropriations for both the army and navy. He also proposed that the production of military aircraft be increased from 12,000 to 50,000 a year.

While the United States began to speed up arms and munitions production, other nations were frantically seeking American arms and supplies. In January a small Dutch military purchasing mission had come to the United States but bought only a few planes and a small amount of military equipment. After the fall of the Netherlands to the Nazis on May 15, the Dutch still had an overseas empire in Southeast Asia—the Netherlands East Indies—to defend against anticipated attack by Germany and an expansionist Japan. On May 19 a purchasing mission from the East Indies came to America and placed an order for more than $50 million worth of planes, tanks, guns, and other arms, as well as tools and materials for producing their own weapons.

Average Americans did not concern themselves with the moral or monetary nuances of arms trade or the financial subtleties of export-import loans. They knew the orders meant jobs. Factories were working overtime. Night shifts were becoming routine. Trucks were rolling. Towns with arsenals and depots, like Rock Island and Schenectady, became boom towns overnight. People were on the move as Americans got down to the crucial business of building a munitions industry. One night in June, 600 heavily loaded freight cars rolled onto the army docks at the Raritan Arsenal in New Jersey. Special shifts of nearly a thousand men worked all night loading 75-millimeter guns, shells and rifles onto barges that would take the munitions to a dozen British ships in nearby New York harbor. On June 11, 1940, the first transfer of American arms and ammunition to Britain took place. The first ship sailed to England two days later. It was the beginning of the policy known as Cash and Carry, soon to be expanded to the Lend-Lease program. The size of orders placed with American industry was staggering. From January 1, 1939, to June 1, 1940,

The Douglas Aircraft plant in Santa Monica (right) was gearing up for increased production, and such airplanes as the giant Pan Am *Yankee Clipper* (below) became emblematic of America's burgeoning industrial strength.

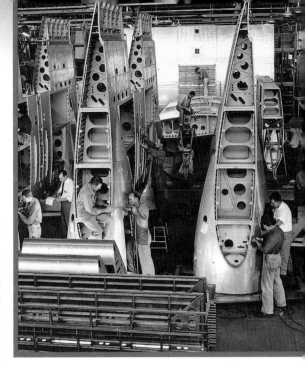

foreign governments placed orders for armaments totaling $600 million. Orders just from June 1 to June 30, 1940, amounted to $800 million. And, in the second half of the year the orders rose by another $1.2 billion. In the last six months of 1940, Congress appropriated $21 billion for national defense, five times the amount appropriated for the entire year of 1939. America had indeed become the "Arsenal of Democracy." And as far as many people were concerned, we were already in the war up to our elbows.

Looking Southward

There was a tremendous increase in air travel in 1940 and 1941. Though much of it was domestic—and much of it related to the booming defense industry—there was also a surge in flights to Central and South America. With war raging in both Europe and the Far East, the tropics became an increasingly popular destination. Pan American World Airways advertised that now, with the new wider, spacious, more streamlined two-engine airplanes replacing the older flying boats, the Caribbean was only seven hours from New York. Pan Am travel posters showing couples relaxing on sandy beaches along with aerial views of the harbor at Rio De Janeiro ("Now only 30 hours from New York") became familiar sights in travel agency windows.

Tropical styles, Cuban heels, and Latin music became popular. Nightclub orchestras played the tango, the bolero, and the rhumba. Noro Morales and his Cuban orchestra had a huge hit with "Vamos a Jugar la Rueda." Expensive hotels and restaurants began to stock tropical fruit, and rum became the drink of the moment. Especially popular was tropical punch—equal parts of white wine and champagne, splashed over a bit of sugar and a pinch of brandy and served in an eight-ounce wine glass with a fat, fresh strawberry floating on top. It was a light, bubbly concoction, perfect for sipping while listening to the gentle harmonies of "I Don't Want to Set the World on Fire" and forgetting the war.

Pan Am had also inaugurated a new southern Pacific route, taking travelers south of Hawaii to Fiji, New Caledonia, and ultimately to New Zealand. In 1940 and 1941, such future battlegrounds as Guam, Midway, and Wake Island were to the average American no more than stops on the new Clipper route.

Fibber McGee and Molly (played by Jim and Marian Jordan), a Thirties radio hit still popular in the early Forties, painted a portrait of a goofy but comfortable home life.

Heroes for an Anxious Time

Americans who couldn't afford air travel could turn to sports for diversion. The last summer before the war was truly a golden age for sports. Joe Louis, Joe DiMaggio, and Ted Williams shared center stage with a three-year-old chestnut stallion named Whirlaway. At the 1941 Kentucky Derby (mint juleps a dollar), Whirly was dead last at the half-mile pole, a good five lengths behind the front-runner. He was still way behind in the final turn. It wasn't until the top of the stretch that Whirlaway's new jockey, young Eddie Arcaro, moved him outside. In a matter of seconds, horse and rider blazed into history.

Writer Red Smith described the race this way: "What he did to those horses was hard to believe even while you were seeing it. He cooked 'em, fried 'em. You could almost hear them sizzle, see them curl like frog legs in the pan." His time of 2 minutes 1.4 seconds was the fastest ever. A week later Whirlaway won the Preakness by five lengths. And on June 7, 1941, he became the fifth Triple Crown winner when he demolished the competition at the Belmont Stakes. In the spring of 1941, with bad news of devastating British losses at Crete—15,000 casualties, including 2,000 sailors drowned when their ships were bombed by the Luftwaffe—Whirlaway became a symbol of pure innocent joy.

A country in need of heroes got them in the persons of Joe Louis and Joe DiMaggio, the sons respectively of a Southern sharecropper and an Italian-born San Francisco fisherman. They were not just extraordinarily gifted athletes, they were quintessentially American antidotes to war-torn Europe and Asia. The Brown Bomber and the Yankee Clipper—each in his own way epitomized the American spirit, each the embodiment of the quiet, determined way the nation went about its business.

On a hazy, hot and humid New York night, June 18, 1941, before a packed Polo Grounds (special blocks of tickets reserved for servicemen), Louis staged an epic battle with Billy Conn, a handsome, cocky, immensely likable, and furiously energetic 23-year-old Irishman from the hardscrabble East Liberty section of Pittsburgh. Conn had been the undisputed light heavyweight champion. At 174 pounds, a good 25 pounds lighter than Louis, he was the lightest challenger for the heavyweight crown since Frenchman Georges Carpentier had fought Jack Dempsey 20 years earlier.

Simply stated, it was one of the greatest fights in boxing history. Conn, a clever boxer, led on points on most cards until he tried to slug it out with the hard-hitting champion in the 13th round. The result was quick and final: a knockout by Louis.

A World Series to Remember

In 1941 baseball was truly the national pastime—as it never had been before and probably never will be again. For two long, lazy months in the last slow, golden American summer before the country went to war, Joe DiMaggio's 56-game hitting streak electrified the nation. Even people who didn't normally follow baseball would check the newspapers "to see if that fellow DiMaggio got a hit." When William Allen White complained that "two-fifths of our people are more interested in baseball than they are in foreign wars," Brooklyn Dodger manager Leo Durocher replied: "He's got it all wrong. It's more like three-fifths." Joe DiMaggio was a majestic, almost magical presence on the diamond. He seemed to perfectly exemplify a quiet ease and graceful, understated elegance. As his roommate, Yankee pitcher and free spirit, Lefty Gomez put it, "He knew that he was DiMaggio, and he knew what that meant to the country."

As the baseball season drew to a close, with Ted Williams of the Boston Red Sox becoming the first player in a decade to hit .400 (on the final day of the season he got six hits in a doubleheader to finish at the .406 mark), a majority of Americans, even in the previously isolationist Midwest, felt that U. S. participation in the war—actually sending our soldiers overseas to fight—was becoming all but inevitable.

The crowds at the 1941 World Series between the Yankees and the Dodgers were more raucous, more high-spirited than usual. All manner of celebrities were on hand, from politicians to movie stars to gangland kingpins. New York Mayor Fiorello LaGuardia, Babe Ruth, Jim Farley and Wendell Wilkie, Joe Louis and Billy Conn, Toots Shor and Frank Costello all rubbed shoulders in the stands.

New York gambler Joe Adonis arrived in a new 1942 Cadillac ("To insure your family's needs for the duration of the emergency," said the ad, "give them a Cadillac."), and the parking lot glistened with the polished chromium of new cars.

Brightening the scene at the ballpark were starlets wearing the new nylons, which were just starting to replace silk stockings, and debutantes with pageboy hairdos, expensive cashmere sweaters, and single strands of pearls, escorted by young men in expensive suits.

President Roosevelt took a break and listened to the entire game on radio. The Yanks won 3-2. It was as if everyone felt that the next World Series would be played in a different and darker world.

And they were right.

Military enlistments began rising in August 1941, when America's eventual entry into the war seemed very likely. After Pearl Harbor young men swamped the recruiting centers (below).

HOMETOWN, USA

I t was the last time most Americans would be on intimate terms with the profound quiet and deep-millpond calm of self-sustaining small-town life. It was the last truly slow time the country would know. Rural America was a smiling land of lush pastures and ripening wheat, of grazing livestock, seed sheds and orchards, of weighing scales and shucking wagons.

The sheet music that wasn't on the piano could be found on the front-porch table along with agricultural magazines, breeder gazettes, and stereopticon slides. It was a time of easy laughter, of yarn-spinning at the general store, of Saturday trips into town, of barbershop shaves and beauty-parlor gossip, of the old swimming hole, and of milk with cream on top. Farm wives cooked for gangs of hired hands at threshing time and washed the cream separator all year-round. Volunteer firemen met at the Grange hall. It was an America of "sociables" and suppers and Sunday best—hilltop churches in midsummer filled with women wearing taffetas, crepes, organdies, and starched ginghams. Pies cooled on the window sills, and the distant barking of a dog was a reminder of how quiet it usually was.

County and state fairs were major social events. One Midwesterner recalls: *The fairs were tent cities and the "streets" were named after famous strains of corn: Golden Dent, Reid's Yellow Dent, Champion White Pearl, St. Charles White, Early Huron, and so forth. Right before the corn-husking contest they would sell switchel—an "old-time replenishing drink" made of molasses and water, seasoned with ginger and vinegar. My grandfather said he would have it as a boy with pieces of johnnycake.*

It was a time that would soon be gone forever.

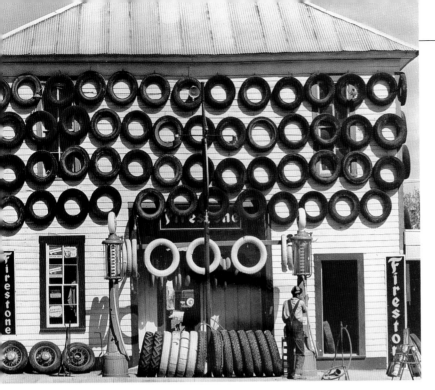

In San Marco, Texas, used tires go begging (left) in the days before wartime rubber rationing.

Below, an Illinois farm family gathers in the parlor at the end of the day. Dad reads the latest edition of *Poultry Keeper* while Mom knits and the boys amuse themselves with tops. The neighbors might stop by later for some singing 'round the pump organ.

In the America of 1940, favorite pastimes included baking cookies in a modern kitchen (left) and playing bingo (below, left) at the county fair at St. Charles, Missouri.

The 1941 California State Picnic in Long Beach attracted more than 40,000 people for such events as a hog-calling contest. Below are the finalists from the contest's more than 500 entrants.

BIJOU
THE DEVIL AND MISS JONES
ALSO THIEVES FALL OUT

DELIGHTFUL
UNINCORPORATED

The general store was still a fixture across the American landscape in 1940. At left, Virginia state senator Loving chatted stoveside with a customer at the senator's Hot Springs emporium.

The streets of Hot Springs, Virginia, were quiet in the early '40s (opposite). It was a time for a snack at the lunch counter (opposite, above) and cones by the side of the road (opposite, below). Nearly every small town had a local Bijou that featured the latest Hollywood offerings (opposite, bottom left).

Cheerful order in the classroom (top) and joyous release at the end of the day (above) marked schooldays in the Forties. Friends, Fido, and fishing (left) could happily consume an entire summer afternoon.

THE PROMISE OF GOOD TIMES

During the second half of 1940, America was rapidly building a nationwide munitions industry—and a new middle class. For the first time in a decade, average Americans had money to spend. Many remember Christmastime 1940 as one of their happiest holidays. *The New York Times* declared: "Gift buying in department stores was an orgy of spending, as if customers were determined to show there was at least one country on earth that enjoyed peace and good will."

The new affluence created something novel in Christmas marketing: the mass merchandising of a comic book hero. Superman, created by Jerry Siegel and Joe Shuster, two cartoonists from Cleveland, had already been the most popular balloon (filled with $1,000 worth of helium) in the Macy's Thanksgiving Day Parade in New York. Then came Superman costumes, Superman underwear, Superman raincoats, and sweatshirts. Behind these rolled toy tanks, jigsaw puzzles, coloring books, pins, lunchboxes, bookbags, and cutout dolls, all featuring the trademark red *S*, the cape and the tights.

One reporter remembered those halcyon days when people never worried about where their next dollar was coming from: *My father was neither a baseball fan nor a supporter of anything Russian. He hated Communism; he was a devout Irish Catholic. But during Joe DiMaggio's 56-game streak and right after the Nazis invaded the Soviet Union, he would toast DiMaggio with vodka, which I can't remember him ever drinking before. He would say, "Joltin' Joe and to hell with Hitler," and throw back a shot. Then he'd say, "You kids want to go to the movies?" Of course we always did. I probably went to more movies that summer than any other time in my life. My sisters and I must've seen One Night in Lisbon ten times. He never worried about money. He always said: "Who knows what's going to happen next year?" And of course he was right.*

The Lindy was still popular at the 1941 Horse Show Ball at the Waldorf-Astoria (left). An evening of dancing was within the reach of many. Above, Freddy Martin and his orchestra entertain a crowded ballroom.

Movie fan magazines played up California as a playground for the rich and famous (below, right). But in the early 1940s, the Golden State's delightful weather and relaxed way of life attracted increasing numbers of ordinary people, and the state's population grew accordingly.

Amusement parks and beaches filled up in the summer of 1940. Above, Luna Park lights up Coney Island; below, the solidly packed beach. Rides like the rotating discs on the Steel Pier at Atlantic City (inset, below) became more mechanically sophisticated. But the main attractions were the cooling sea breezes, the undulating surf, and the fun of being part of a large and joyful crowd.

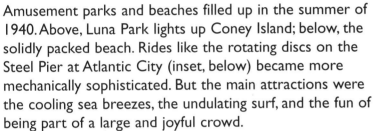

Ted Williams (left) brought such grace and intelligence to the game of baseball that it became possible to talk seriously about the science of hitting. Fans flocked to ballparks, as much, it seemed, to jeer the umpires and boo the opposing team as to cheer the home team. Above, fans deliver Bronx cheers at Yankee Stadium.

Sports journalism and broadcasting of the 1940s portrayed athletes as persons as well as heroes. Even the great racehorse Whirlaway (below, leading the pack at the Preakness) was given a personality. Radio, especially, allowed fans to follow the exploits of figures like Leroy "Satchel" Paige (below, right), the great pitcher of the Kansas City Monarchs of the Negro League, and Tom Harmon (bottom, running with football) as he led the Michigan Wolverines to victory over Illinois in a rock 'em, sock 'em Big Ten contest.

Rita Hayworth—born Margarita Carmen Cansino—had been a Spanish dancer since the age of twelve. After dying her hair auburn and changing her name, she became one of the biggest movie stars of the Forties and a favorite pinup of American servicemen. Musicals like Jerome Kern's *You Were Never Lovelier,* 1942, also featuring Fred Astaire, and *Cover Girl,* 1944, used her dancing talent to the fullest. Meanwhile, the Hollywood boom of the late 1930s continued into the Forties with films like *Now Voyager* (below) starring Paul Henreid (who costarred in *Casablanca)* and Bette Davis, already a winner of two Academy Awards.

The Hollywood premier, a staple of the fan magazines, became even more lavish when used as a fund raiser for war relief. At right, Clark Gable and his wife, Carole Lombard, attend a premier at Grauman's Chinese Theatre for Greek War Relief in the winter of 1941.

The Hollywood studios were in their heyday in the 1940s in spite of continued efforts by stars to break their contracts and be free of the studios. Bette Davis fought a bitter and ultimately losing battle with Warner Brothers. Judy Garland made six films for MGM between 1938 and 1946, each an arduous song-and-dance extravaganza. In Busby Berkeley's *For Me and My Gal,* Garland earned top billing over male stars George Murphy and Gene Kelly. (As early as the late Forties, Garland was exhausted and developed serious health problems.)

Thomas "Fats" Waller (right) combined musical genius and a comical manner. He produced hundreds of recordings from 1919 to 1943, including hits like "Honeysuckle Rose" and "Ain't Misbehavin'," and influenced several generations of jazz musicians.

The big band sound, exemplified by the Glenn Miller Orchestra (left), strong enough to come across faithfully over the airwaves, dominated the popular music of the Forties. Even smaller bands, like the ensemble shown playing at the Hickory House on 52nd Street in New York (below) did their best to imitate the Miller sound.

Kay Starr

Growing up on a farm in the Arbuckle Mountains of Oklahoma, all Kay Starr ever wanted was to be a performer. She got her wish, singing with the big bands of Glenn Miller and Charlie Barnett.

Part Cherokee (although people kept telling her she looked Italian), Starr got her big break with Glenn Miller in the early '40s. She remembers:

That music was so important, I really felt in my heart of hearts that the era that I was born into was the best....We had the best of everything. We had the best motion pictures. We had the best movie stars. We had the best stories. We had the best music. We had the best bands. You name anything that was entertainment that we didn't have the best of. People...had a good time. And what did it cost you to go and dance all night long with somebody you cared about? Hey, there's nothing bad about having somebody have their arms around you and you're dancing. The songs at that point were like stories. They were like poems. They had a beginning and a middle and an end.

When she traveled with the band during the war, she helped the musicians make the best of difficult times.

It was difficult during the war to get things cleaned quickly, to get laundry done quickly. Sometimes those guys would come in, and if you were downwind of 'em, you could hardly get your breath.... I did make a deal with those musicians. If they would just wash their shirts, I would iron the front. I said, "I'll come in an hour early and I will iron your shirt." And I used to iron the cuffs and the sleeves up to the elbow. And I'd do the front. I didn't do the back; nobody saw that. Those are the things that singers do if they're part of a band they love.

After the war, the soldiers came home and a strange sadness set in. The reality of the homecoming was not what most had dreamed of.

You didn't stay naive during the war. My husband came back. He was the first trumpet player for NBC. And they had promised all the musicians who left that when they came back they would have their jobs. Well, it was not true. And my husband became very angry, as so many men did... the people that ran big companies and everything had to have somebody in there to run it. They couldn't...women couldn't do everything, you know.

So they had gotten so used to those people, young minds, the energy of young people, that they were hesitant to take back these so-called "war-torn souls." My husband was so angry and he was so mad all the time that I couldn't live with him. So I had to divorce him. Now, that was another tragedy of the war.

THE TEENAGERS

It might be stretching it, but one could point to the jitterbug as the first indication of the existence of a youth counterculture in America. For the first time, teenagers not only had their own dance but also their own uniform for celebrating with reckless abandon: saddle shoes, oversize multiprint skirts, and pegged pants. And, in the most extreme cases, the zoot suits with their accompanying accouterments: the wide-brimmed hat, the long watch chain and the ducktail haircut.

In metropolitan areas, teen "nightclubs" (which copied the adult establishments but served only nonalcoholic beverages) began to appear. A Connecticut youth remembered starting one:

My brother had been to real nightclubs in New York and told me about them. And of course we'd all seen the movies with their Art Deco bars, shiny dance floors, and plush decor. We knew there had to be a light on every table. And we had the oversize menus, even though all we served was soda.

We played Duke Ellington records. "Take the A Train," "C-Jam Blues," "Chelsea Bridge," "Don't Get Around Much Anymore." So we called the place the Top Hat. After the war started, we called it The Top Hat Canteen.

In 1940 Frank Sinatra placed 22nd in *Billboard* magazine's Collegiate Choice popularity poll of male vocalists. The magazine called him a good ballad singer but claimed he was "nil on showmanship." A year later he was the most popular singer in the country. His legendary appearances at the Paramount Theater in New York, and a less well known stint at the Riobamba

Club had created the entirely new phenomenon of the teen idol. America was filled with young women afflicted with "Sinatra-itis," who would go into "Sinatrances" whenever they heard "Swoonatra" sing.

When Ben Gross, radio editor of the New York *Daily News*, wrote that he did not consider young Blue Eyes to be the best singer in the world, the reaction from fans was swift and unequivocal: "You should burn in oil, pegs should be driven into your body, and you should be hung by your thumbs," wrote one furious fan. And another wrote: "I'd love to take you to Africa, tie you to the gound, and pour honey on you and let the ants bite you to pieces."

So began America's first fanatical teenage movement.

Teenagers had never exerted the kind of influence over the popular culture that they did in the '40s. The zany exuberance of youth (far left) became the basis for national fads. Zoot suits (left) and bobby sox were emblematic of the times.

Teenagers could do more in the Forties because they had more money and more things to spend it on. Cars of the previous decade, like the jalopy with a rumble seat (right), were within their grasp. And cheap gasoline helped make automobile excursions a popular pastime.

Frank Sinatra's fans, like these enthusiastic young women outside New York's Paramount Theater, came in droves to hear the Voice. (A fan magazine distributed "anti-swoon mints" to everyone waiting in line.) At far left, Sinatra as he appeared in a movie of the early 1940s. It was then widely expected that Sinatra's career would fade as he became older.

Throughout the country civic groups sought to harness the energy of teenagers by sponsoring Teen Frolics and hiring big bands like Benny Goodman's. Below, bobby soxers clutch photos of the King of Swing, while waiting for an autograph.

Zoot suits came to the United States in the Thirties by way of England and caught on with teens, who thought they made them look older. Wartime restrictions on fabric made zoot suits unpopular, and they became identified with draft dodging. Right, a still from the film *Hit Parade of 1943*.

The Andrews Sisters (Laverne, Maxine and Patti), one of the most popular singing groups among teenagers in the Forties, first sang on radio with singer-bandleader Dick Haymes (left). During the war the trio starred in films like *Buck Privates* (1941) and *Follow the Boys* (1944) and traveled extensively entertaining the troops. Young men regarded Bing Crosby (below, left) as a role model, although he was already 36 in 1940, fresh off his Thirties hits, "White Christmas" and "Silent Night." Crosby's popularity in radio and movies soared later in the Forties.

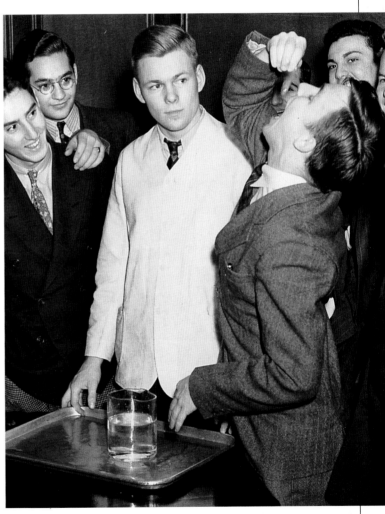

College students in the early Forties earned a reputation for silliness with stunts like goldfish-swallowing, practiced above by the reputed originator of the fad, Harvard freshman Lothrop Withington Jr. However, polls revealed that most students, like those at the soda fountain at left, were fairly conservative. Fewer than 40 percent of students polled in 1940 approved of sex before marriage.

BRIGHT LIGHTS AND HARD TIMES

The advice offered in a sporting goods catalog issued in the summer of 1941—"There has never been a summer when it is so important to relax. The deluge is coming, so dress up and play."—perfectly reflected the giddy, heady, who-knows-what-tomorrow-will-bring mood of America in 1941. It was a bright-lights-big-city time of fast and easy night life; of what've we got to lose; of why not, instead of why.

The emphasis on glamorous sexuality was epitomized by the famous *Life* magazine photo of a young and on-the-way-up Rita Hayworth wearing a slinky nightgown of satin and lace, kneeling invitingly on a bed. Sales of women's underwear soared in the 12 months before Pearl Harbor. One company, Blue Swan Mills, sponsored a panty-of-the-month club—a favorite was a step-in with "You Hoo" lettered on the thigh.

The early Forties was the golden age of sleek evening dresses, designed for night-clubbing at 21, the Stork Club, El Morocco, El Gaucho, Leon and Eddie's, the Copacabana, the Latin Quarter, and Toots Shor's.

One defense worker at the Raritan Arsenal in New Jersey remembered a night out with a soldier:

He was a captain from Santa Cruz, California, named Andrew. Very nice. Very sweet. He was leaving in four or five days. His last Saturday we went to 21 and El Morocco. I remember that I wore a very pretty pink suit. It was very soft like a plush, but it wasn't velvet, just a fine wool suit. White blouse. Black leather pumps. Black bag. When we were coming back, Penn Station was packed, full of people like us who missed the last train and had to wait till morning. The atmosphere was festive— everyone was talking and laughing, as if we were all part of the same big party.

New York became the world center of nightlife in the early Forties for the simple reason that all the great cities of Europe were blacked-out at night. The number of nightclubs was dizzying, and the wealthy came from every corner of the globe to party in Gotham's swank clubs. Far left, the main dining room at the Copacabana. Above, left, the sons of William Randolph Hearst dine at the Stork Club. Above, right, Stork Club owner Sherman Billingsley reluctantly closes the club in compliance with the wartime curfew. At left, society figure Mabel Boll, dubbed the Diamond Queen by the newspapers, dines with friends at El Morocco.

Much-married socialite Barbara Hutton (left) attends a tennis match in Palm Beach, Florida, in the winter of 1940-41. Below, debutantes dance the Flower Waltz at the Coty Debutante Cotillion at the Waldorf-Astoria. In the 1940s many Americans enjoyed an opulence not seen since the Roaring Twenties.

Women began to play richer movie roles in the '40s more reflective of modern life. Left, Katharine Hepburn as the complex Tracy Lord in *The Philadelphia Story*, and, below, Dorothy Comingore as Susan, the bored and unhappy wife in *Citizen Kane*. Flamboyant actress Marlene Dietrich is shown below, left, in a characteristic pose in 1941. Thanks to Dietrich and other Hollywood divas, public smoking and the wearing of slacks became acceptable for women during the 1940s.

On a chilly April day in 1939, Marian Anderson sang at the Lincoln Memorial in Washington. The concert was arranged by Eleanor Roosevelt after Anderson was denied use of Constitution Hall by the Daughters of the American Revolution. The event was more than an artistic triumph: it brought the issue of racial equality to the forefront of America's consciousness.

For much of America, the Depression was slow in passing. These two 1939 photographs, the one at left taken in downtown Los Angeles and the other, above, in a subway car in New York City, appeared widely in the early Forties and served to prove that many Americans were still experiencing hard times.

By 1940, more than 350,000 families of migrant workers, most of them black, were crisscrossing the country in search of work. Very little of the New Deal had addressed their needs. Below, as late as 1945, remnants of the right-wing group America First, stilled by Pearl Harbor, were still actively seeking to limit immigration and impede integration in war factories. Below, their rallies were picketed by civil rights and labor organizations.

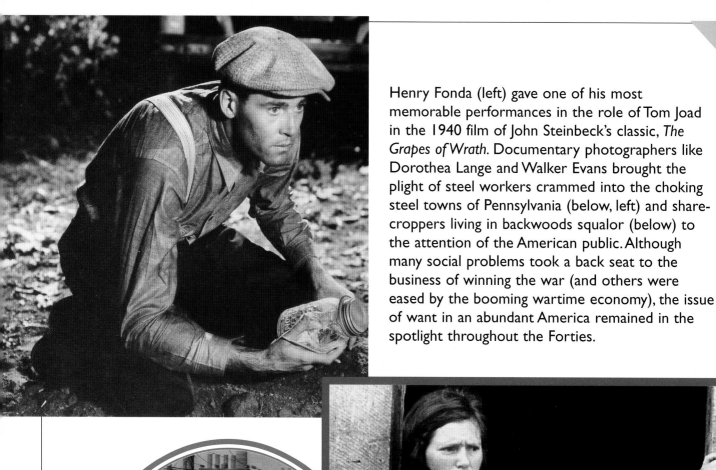

Henry Fonda (left) gave one of his most memorable performances in the role of Tom Joad in the 1940 film of John Steinbeck's classic, *The Grapes of Wrath*. Documentary photographers like Dorothea Lange and Walker Evans brought the plight of steel workers crammed into the choking steel towns of Pennsylvania (below, left) and share-croppers living in backwoods squalor (below) to the attention of the American public. Although many social problems took a back seat to the business of winning the war (and others were eased by the booming wartime economy), the issue of want in an abundant America remained in the spotlight throughout the Forties.

Paul J. Moore

After attending St. Paul's School and Yale University, Paul Moore joined the Marine Corps and fought at Guadalcanal, where he was wounded.

After the war, he attended divinity school on the GI Bill. He eventually became the Episcopal bishop of New York.

Moore remembers his conflicting feelings about being wealthy during the Depression years.

I had a wonderful childhood. I didn't realize it was so different, but I had my own pony. There were two butlers and a house man on the staff, plus an upstairs maid and a downstairs maid, and two kitchen maids, and a cook, two chauffeurs, a custom-made Rolls-Royce, which I was so embarrassed to ride in when we rode through Hoboken. We'd see all the bread lines, people selling apples, and I used to duck down underneath the seats so I wouldn't be seen. I guess that was my first conflict about having a lot of money.

Having fought in the Pacific, he recalled the brutality of the battlefield, as well as its special brand of camaraderie.

I loved the Marines...obviously I didn't like the life, but my friends. You actually see people giving up their lives, risking their lives for their brothers. It was an extraordinary kind of heroism...as well as a lot of very bad stuff. I remember one full colonel...We were preparing to defend a stretch of battleground called Bloody Ridge. The colonel's idea was to put Japanese corpses into foxholes. I remember his riding along the top of this ridge in a jeep, with a rope out the back tied around a Japanese corpse, one of those disfigured corpses, and he was driving as fast as he could and laughing. The Japanese when they attacked would come up the hill and see their friends bloated and dead. I mean that... that's not very romantic.

We used to talk about our family and our girlfriends and what meal we would have when we first came to the States—that was a big topic of conversation. "Well, I'm going to have a hamburger" or "I'm going to have spaghetti" or whatever it was. Long, long talks about what you would have and how many drinks you'd have and where your favorite bar was.

After he was wounded, Moore was sent home and put on tour selling war bonds.

When I came back from overseas I had to address war plants...and here I was, a big peace person over the last several years. Well, there I was with my Marine uniform, Navy Cross, Silver Star, Purple Heart, and rifle medals, and a thousand people out there on their lunch break at a munitions factory, and me standing up, giving this speech. They gave me a hand grenade and I held it up and yelled: "You've got to make a whole lot more of these if we're gonna get our boys home."

WAR DRAWS NEAR

On March 15, 1941, four days after President Roosevelt signed the Lend-Lease Act, he spoke at the annual White House Correspondents' Association dinner. The president told the gathering—and in effect all Americans—that the days ahead would be difficult. "Whether you are in the armed services, or whether you are a steel worker or a stevedore, a machinist or a housewife, a farmer or a banker, a storekeeper or a manufacturer—to all of you it will mean sacrifices."

But he ended by saying: "Never, in all our history...have Americans faced a task so well worthwhile. May it be said of us in the days to come that our children and our children's children will rise up and call us blessed." Though not a call to arms, the speech was definitely a call to duty. Veteran columnist Raymond Clapper later said: "Everyone who was in the room must have heard the leaf of history turning. Twenty years of isolationism gone. We sought a life where we could shut out the ugly world, but we found we could not stay there."

Throughout the spring and summer of 1941, relations between the United States and Germany deteriorated. The *Baltimore Sun* reported that one day when the German consulate in San Francisco unfurled a four-foot by eight-foot swastika from its ninth-story offices, not only did an angry crowd gather in the street below to boo and jeer, but the manager of the store across the street retaliated by hanging an even larger American flag. Then two sailors climbed the fire escape, and one of them succeeded in ripping the swastika in half. Afterward the sailor told reporters: "I couldn't let that flag stay up there. It was up to someone to get it down, so I just went up there."

When isolationist Charles A. Lindbergh spoke on September 11, in Des Moines, Iowa, he told a mostly sympathetic crowd: "The three most important groups which have been pressing this country toward war are the British, the Jewish, and the Roosevelt administration." But a high school student remembers: "When I heard that, all I could think was: It's not the British, the Jewish, or the Roosevelt administration that's firing torpedoes at American ships. It's the Nazis."

A week earlier, an American destroyer had been attacked, The freighter *Steel Seafarer* had been sunk on September 7; and another ship four days later. The next day, President Roosevelt told the country that the United States Navy now had orders to shoot whenever threatened. War with Hitler seemed unavoidable.

By this time, the situation with Japan had also deteriorated. On October 17, Gen. Hideki Tojo became prime minister; most Americans believed that meant war with Japan was imminent. Still, some isolationists stuck to their guns. On October 27, the *Chicago Tribune* editorialized: "What vital interest of the U.S. can Japan threaten? She cannot attack us. That is a military impossibility. Even our base at Hawaii is beyond the effective striking power of her fleet."

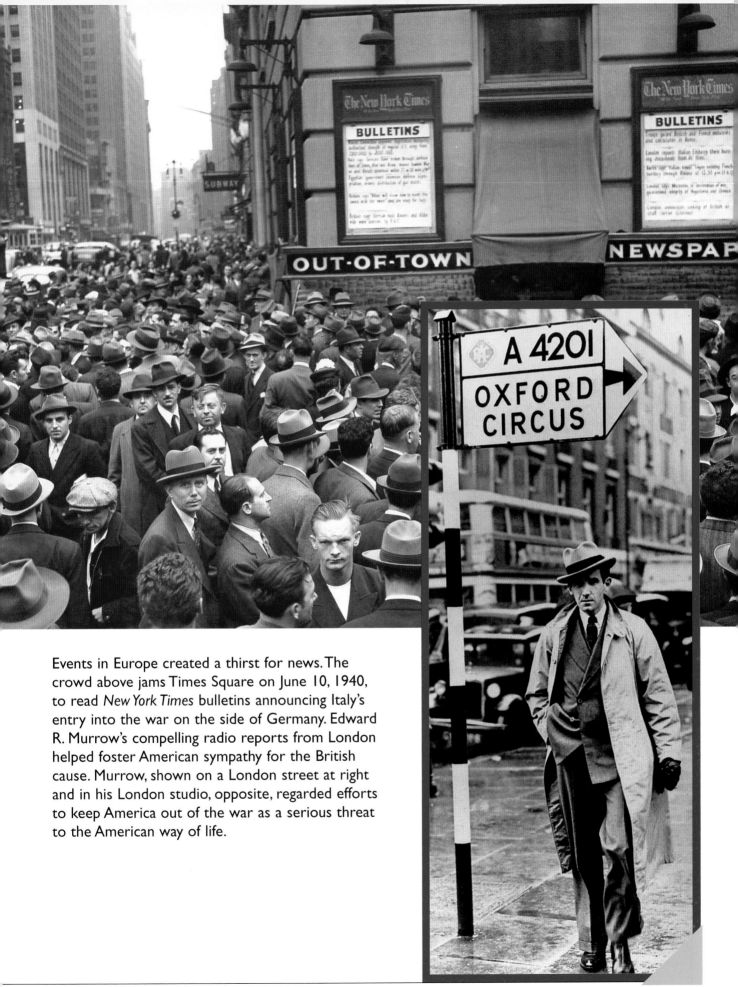

Events in Europe created a thirst for news. The crowd above jams Times Square on June 10, 1940, to read *New York Times* bulletins announcing Italy's entry into the war on the side of Germany. Edward R. Murrow's compelling radio reports from London helped foster American sympathy for the British cause. Murrow, shown on a London street at right and in his London studio, opposite, regarded efforts to keep America out of the war as a serious threat to the American way of life.

The easy rapport between Prime Minister Winston Churchill and President Franklin D. Roosevelt (shown above at a wartime conference in 1942) played an important role in maintaining amicable British-American relations. The 1939 state visit by Britain's King George and Queen Elizabeth to the United States helped strengthen the already close ties between the two nations.

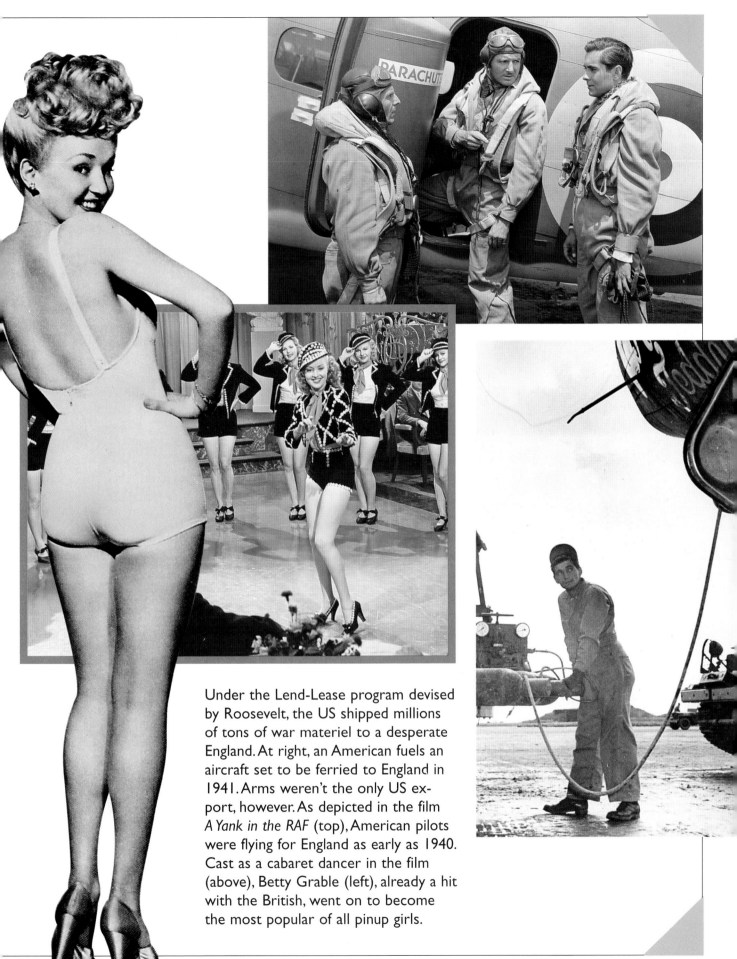

Under the Lend-Lease program devised by Roosevelt, the US shipped millions of tons of war materiel to a desperate England. At right, an American fuels an aircraft set to be ferried to England in 1941. Arms weren't the only US export, however. As depicted in the film *A Yank in the RAF* (top), American pilots were flying for England as early as 1940. Cast as a cabaret dancer in the film (above), Betty Grable (left), already a hit with the British, went on to become the most popular of all pinup girls.

Americans took a keen interest in the progress of the war in Europe (top), and sympathies understandably lay with the nations that fell before the Nazi war machine. The ease with which Germany defeated France was particularly unsettling. Americans were shocked by photos of Wehrmacht troops marching past the Arc de Triomphe in Paris (left) and moved by the image, above, of a Frenchman crying as he watches the Germans entering Marseilles.

Rudy Salas

Rudy Salas, now an artist and muralist living in Hacienda Heights, California, was seventeen years old and living in South Central Los Angeles when World War II began. He worked as a day laborer in an aircraft plant, where he made the money he needed to buy a zoot suit, the uniform of the Mexican-American street gangs of Los Angeles. Street fights were frequent between gang members and servicemen based in the area. But Salas was unscathed by any of these incidents, and later went on to work for the City of Los Angeles as a painter and muralist.

The activities of the gangs during that era, says Salas, often involved more posturing than violence. Rudy recalls one unexpected incident, however:

The gang that I was from hung around in front of the pool hall on Central Avenue in LA. On one block there was a pool hall—it was a hot dog restaurant called The Coney Island. And we all knew each other. We knew the pool hall people...the people from the Coney Island. And we were very angry and shocked when the beautiful Coney Island was closed because the owners were Japanese—Mary, her mother, her father, and then...what's his name, Kuto...when they were shipped off, you know, to the internment camp. We couldn't understand what the hell was going on.

Like many people who remember the Forties, Salas has special memories of the music of the time.

Oh, Lionel Hampton...I remember seeing him...At one time he had a big hit called "Flying Home." He'd be playing on the stage at the Paramount Theater ...the house would be packed, rocking. Then they'd start playing "Flying Home" and everybody just started jumping all over the place and rocking and everything. The screen in the background would light up and they would show a film of these old planes, flying, zooming toward the camera...it was hypnotic because it'd make everybody go crazy. You'd see the band playing and the planes coming at you and you're jumping around and people dancing in the aisles and all happy...It was great.

For Rudy, life on the home front in wartime mixed relief with disappointment.

It wasn't anything about patriotism, you know. No, to me it was you're going off, you know, going over, an adventure, a macho trip. Then along came the LAPD and did me a big favor: they punched in my eardrum. So when I went for induction, they turned me away. This is embarrassing, but it took me a long time to get over it. We were 4-F...4-F guys walking around while all those other guys were out there dying.

Timescope

U.S. Population
(in millions)

1930	122.7
1940	**132.1**
1950	**150.7**
1990	250.4

Percentage Urban / Percentage Rural

1930	56.1 / 43.9
1940	**56.5 / 43.5**
1950	**64.0 / 36.0**
1990	74.9 / 27.2

Average Number of People Per Household

1930	3.89
1940	**3.67**
1950	**3.37**
1990	2.62

Shopping in 1940

Newspapers: Daily, Sunday	3 cents
Women's Suits	10 cents
Men's Suits	$15
Gin (1/5 bottle)	$20-$29.50
Broadway Tickets	$0.99
Skis	$0.55-$3.30
Spin-dry Washers	$12.94
Monthly Rental, 4-room Apartment, West 72nd St, New York City	$59.95
Men's Shoes	$105
Men's Shirts	$7.95-$9.95
Radio Console	$1.25-$3.85
Bar of Soap	$39.95
	2.5 cents

Median Annual Income, 1941:
$2,000

Tax Freedom Day
(Day of the year on which all tax obligations to the government are paid off)

1930	February 9
1940	**March 8**
1950	**April 3**
1960	April 17
1990	May 5

...ffo at the Box Office

Money-Grossing Stars–1941

1. Mickey Rooney
2. Clark Gable
3. Abbott and Costello (left)
4. Bob Hope
5. Spencer Tracy

Money-Grossing Stars–1943

1. Betty Grable
2. Bob Hope
3. Abbott and Costello
4. Bing Crosby
5. Gary Cooper

Radio Favorites—1940

Favorite Programs

1. Jack Benny
2. Fred Allen
3. Information Please
4. Bob Hope
5. Bing Crosby

Favorite Quiz Program

1. Information Please
2. Take it or Leave it
3. Truth or Consequences
4. Quiz Kids (below)
5. Kay Kyser

Favorite Dramatic Program

1. Lux Radio Theater
2. Helen Hayes
3. One Man's Family
4. Arch Obeler
5. Columbia Workshop

Legacy of the Early Forties

Jeep	
M&M's Candy	
Dacron	1940
Cheerios	1940
Wonder Woman	1941
Bazooka Rocket Gun	1941
18-Year Old Vote (Georgia)	1941
Jefferson Memorial	1942
Chiquita Banana	1943
Seventeen Magazine	1943
Frozen Orange Juice	1944
Tupperware	1944
	1945
	1945

The Japanese attack on Pearl Harbor on December 7, 1941, came after months of US Navy maneuvers aimed at minimizing the damage from a possible attack on the base. Above, the attack while it was in progress (one of the few color photographs taken). At right, defense workers in Philadelphia attend the opening ceremonies of an armor plating plant in June 1941. It was clear to everyone that summer that American industry was going to be vital if this country ever became involved in the war.

December 7, 1941. On that day, a foreign military force attacked US soil for the first time in more than 125 years. The country was at war. In the next four years, virtually every aspect of American life would undergo profound and lasting change. The United States that existed on Saturday night, December 6, 1941, was gone forever.

Hawaii is farther from Japan than our Atlantic coastline is from Europe. If oceans really were the natural protective boundaries that many believed they were, then the attack on Pearl Harbor should not have happened. The Japanese bombs that fell on Oahu shattered the last illusion of the isolationists. They also destroyed differences and dissension among the American people. There was an immediate consolidation of the nation's will. Unity was achieved overnight.

"White House says Japs attack Pearl Harbor" flashed over the newswires at 2:25 PM Eastern Standard Time. *Time* magazine reported that in a theater in Dallas, 2,000 people were watching Gary Cooper in *Sergeant York* when the news was announced. There was a pause. Then a few stunned seconds of absolute silence—and then loud shouting and exuberant yells. Most of the country reacted in a similar manner: disbelief, stunned silence, then an unbridled rush of American energy.

The War Arrives on the Airwaves

That night, almost everyone was glued to the radio while President Roosevelt conferred with his closest advisers. The sounds of Jack Benny and Edgar Bergen and Charlie McCarthy were particularly reassuring that night, and in homes everywhere people kept asking, "Is there any news?" Later that evening, First Lady Eleanor Roosevelt made a special broadcast to the women of America:

"I have a boy at sea on a destroyer—for all I know he may be on his way to the Pacific; two of my children are in coast cities on the Pacific. Many of you all over the country have boys in the service

THE HOME FRONT
America in World War II

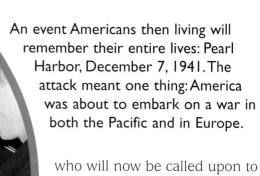

An event Americans then living will remember their entire lives: Pearl Harbor, December 7, 1941. The attack meant one thing: America was about to embark on a war in both the Pacific and in Europe.

who will now be called upon to go into action; you have friends and families in what has become a danger zone. You cannot escape anxiety, you cannot escape the clutch of fear at your heart, and yet I hope that the certainty of what we have to meet will make you rise above those fears....I feel as though I were standing upon a rock, and that rock is my faith in my fellow citizens."

Most Americans experienced an unfamiliar mixture of shock, deep sorrow, fear, fierce anger, grim determination, and feverish energy. While Mrs. Roosevelt's words were being broadcast from Washington, FBI agents throughout the country were systematically rounding up any Japanese considered to be dangerous. In New York City, this meant the arrest of Japan's Consul General Morishima Morito, whose briefcase was found to contain 20 rolls of film that included shots of the Manhattan skyline and every bridge leading in and out of the city.

In White Plains, New York, a Japanese janitor named Matsuabo Matushita (a Brooklyn Dodger fan with a fondness for spaghetti) made an abortive attempt at hara-kiri. "My country," he said, "has done wrong in attacking the United States." (His wounds were not serious.) Japanese-Americans everywhere were feeling fearful and anxious, emotions that would haunt them for the rest of the war. That night, comedian Bert Wheeler introduced the first anti-Japanese song of the war: "We'll Knock the Japs Right Into the Laps of the Nazis."

We didn't want to do it but they're asking for it now,
So we'll knock the Japs right into the laps of the Nazis.
When they hop on Honolulu, that's a thing we won't allow,
So we'll knock the Japs right into the laps of the Nazis.

By the time Congress formally declared war the next day, two other new songs had appeared: "The Sun Will Be Setting on the Land of the Rising Sun" and "You're a Sap, Mr. Jap."

..we here highly resolve that these dead shall not have died in vain...

REMEMBER DEC. 7th!

Pitching In on the Home Front

America during wartime was blackouts and brownouts and dimouts. It was gasoline rationing (with A, B, and C windshield stickers), and swing bands at noontime war bond rallies. Many women rolled bandages two days a week at the Elks Club; an eight-year-old girl sold newspapers in Pittsburgh; and Gen. George C. Marshall came to New York to unveil the country's largest USO sign ("USO deserves the support of every individual citizen"). Wheat flourished on the Dakota prairies and peanuts were stacked like hay in eastern North Carolina. People everywhere were involved in Civil Air Patrol or blood banks or victory gardens. (At their peak, some 20 million victory gardens produced 40 percent of all vegetables grown in the United States.) It was "We're in it—Let's win it," and "Back the attack—With War Bonds." Babies' nipples were made smaller to save rubber, and liquor distillers voluntarily converted their plants to the manufacture of ethyl alcohol for war purposes. It was a time of gold-star mothers and bereaved families. Playing pinball machines, roller skating, and duckpin bowling; *Information Please* on the radio, buffaloburgers in New York, a 12-year-old girl raising the flag at the post office in Luray, Virginia, and "America Calling, Take Your Place in Civilian Defense." Parlor games grew in popularity (a 1942 survey reported that cards were played in 87 percent of American homes).

It was "Grow More in '44" and "Try and Buy a Retread." It was a time of coffee and sugar rationing. The Schrafft's restaurant chain brought back the honey-and-molasses coconut kisses it had introduced during the sugar shortage of World War I. America during wartime was a block service leader's instruction kit with a suggested speech:

Good afternoon, Mrs. Smith. I am Mary Jones of 142 East 72nd Street, one of your neighbors, and a member of your local War Council's Block Leader Service. I am called a Block Service Leader. I am calling upon you today particularly in reference to the Food Rationing Project about which you probably have read. Is there any information about this project or any other matter that I can give you that will be helpful?

High school students read *Guadalcanal Diary* and *They Were Expendable*, and most could tell you that Aunt Jemima was the nickname for a high explosive (mixed with flour) that Americans were smuggling to Chinese saboteurs behind Japanese lines. The WPB (War Production Board) and the OPA (Office of Price Administration) became important in people's lives. The language was enlivened with such new terms as *GI* and *dogface*, *gung ho* and *gooney bird*, *V-mail* and *Dear John letter*, *jerry can* and *jungle juice*, *snow job* and *SOP* ("standard operating procedure").

And Hollywood constantly reminded Americans that it was a people's war we were fighting:

> *"This is the war of all the people. It must be fought in the factories, fought in the hearts of every man and child who loves freedom. This is the people's war. This is our war."*
>
> (Mrs. Miniver, 1942)

> *"All people will learn that and come to see that wars do not have to be. We will make this the last war; we will make a free world for all men. The earth belongs to us the people. If we fight for it."*
>
> (So Proudly We Hail, 1943)

Into the Factories

America during wartime was women in California at the stamping machines in the aircraft factories and behind the wheels of taxicabs. All across the land women drove trucks—and maintained and repaired them. Women were welders, crane operators, shell loaders, section hands, coal mine checkers, train conductors, lumberjacks, cowgirls, and barbers. They ran elevators, piloted ferries, and operated hydraulic presses. They danced with soldiers in the Bamboo Room till well past one—but at eight the next morning they were punching a clock or washing a car or teaching school or packing shrimp or at the cashier's window, or firing a gun at the Aberdeen Proving Ground. In Bridegeport, Connecticut, one ordnance plant actively recruited women with an all-out campaign featuring the slogan, "If you can drive a car, you can run a machine." Women made up 12 percent of the work force in shipyards (mostly on the East Coast) and 10 percent in aircraft assembly plants

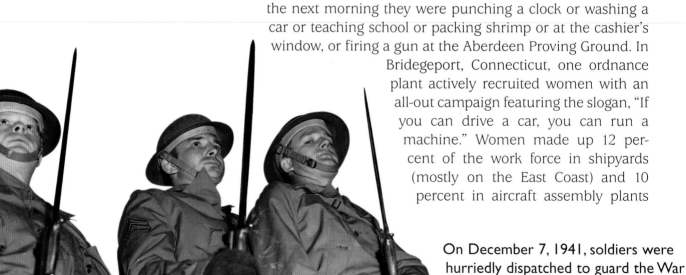

On December 7, 1941, soldiers were hurriedly dispatched to guard the War Department in Washington. They still wore World War I vintage helmets.

A group gathers on the Capitol steps to hear President Roosevelt's announcement of the declaration of war with Japan. Below, trading on the floor of the New York Stock Exchange comes to a halt as traders listen to the president.

(mostly on the West Coast). The Sylvania Electric Company assembly lines for tubes used in the VT proximity fuses relied solely on women. (The reasoning was that their smaller fingers provided greater dexterity in assembling the tiny parts.)

America during wartime was "Let's Go For The Knockout Blow." It was Latin music heard everywhere: "Tico Tico," "Frenesi," "Perfidia," "Siboney," and "Poinciana." As an expression of solidarity with our Asian allies, Chinatowns enjoyed renewed popularity. In San Francisco, Hollywood stars Orson Welles and Rita Hayworth ate chicken with almonds at Johnny Kan's Cathay House, and swarms of sailors at the Li Po Bar listened to Peter Wong sing "What Is This Thing Called Love?" in Chinese. In New York the blackouts were announced in Cantonese, and servicemen on leave ate Chinese-style pineapple spareribs.

America at war was a cornfield turning into a bomber plant, a woodland transformed into a tank arsenal. It was overnight boom town (Phenix City, Alabama) after overnight boom town (Starke, Florida).

A Washington reporter told his readers about one man who rode the boom in a typical wartime jackpot town:

Art Smith used to run a hog ranch in Iowa. In 1889 he sold his ranch, went west, settled in California, bought a hotel, almost went bankrupt, and wondered why he ever left Iowa in the first place. But now, as the jukebox blasts away in the crowded bar of the Hotel Taylor, town of Paso Robles, and as soldiers and civilians stand three deep at the desk clamoring for rooms, he gazes at the spectacle with unbelieving eyes. Paso Robles, midway between San Francisco and Los Angeles and once just an almond-growing town on Route 101, is war-wild. Things began happening to Paso Robles and to Art Smith when construction work started on Camp Roberts thirteen miles to the north. There was only one jewelry shop when the commotion started; now there are six. New beauty parlors opened; so did

JAP... You're Next!

THE MIGHTY 7 WAR LOAN

BUY EXTRA BONDS

Freedom from Fear

radio repair shops, a bowling alley, drive-in restaurants, auto courts, Army and Navy supply stores and the Hong Kong Cafe. Population jumped from 2,800 to 7,000, and Art Smith is only wishing that his Hotel Taylor had an annex. On Saturday evenings the place is besieged—colonels, majors, captains, lieutenants are all turned away. No rooms.

America at war meant Americans on the move. Between Pearl Harbor and V-E Day more than 5 million people left farms to live and work in cities or to work at defense jobs. As people crisscrossed the country, the American roadside became a wonderfully motley reflection of patriotic fervor. There were roadside vendors, young and old, sitting beside highways peddling everything from baby chicks and cactus to pecans and puppies. On Route 35 in New Jersey, amid the smell of salt air, the sheet-music man sold lyrics to patriotic songs—not just "God Bless America," "Praise the Lord and Pass the Ammunition," and "I Left My Heart at the Stage Door Canteen," but "Goodbye, Momma, I'm Off to Yokahama," "Let's Knock the Hit out of Hitler," and "When Those Little Yellow Bellies Meet the Cohens and the Kelleys."

Roadside America meant roadside food. You could get a bowl of Slap-the-Jap Chili at the Best Yet Cafe in Colorado City, Texas (just west of Abilene). "Good Food in a Country Town," promised the Brookside Grill in Bryson City, North Carolina. Mac's Cake and Malt Shop in Seligman, Arizona, made no mention of food, only "New Beds and Gas Heat," but inside soldiers were eating doughnuts and listening to "Milkman, Keep Those Bottles Quiet" on the radio. "Tequila Rag" was on the jukebox while a soldier was having a double-decker sandwich in the Hi-Way Cafe on Route 90 in Sanderson, Texas. Charlie's Foghorn in Steamboat Springs, Colorado, had a daily "Taps for the Japs" luncheon special; the Out-of-the-Sea-and-Into-the-Pan grill on Long Island had a flag, a "Loose Lips Sink Ships" poster, and clippings about U-boats on the walls.

In 1940 the United States built 346 tanks; in 1942, 24,000. Who was going to drive all those tanks? Maj. Gen. Alvin C. Gillem gave a reporter this answer: "Now put a taxi driver from New York or Chicago in one of those tanks and there's nothing that can stop him. The Germans and Japs will find that out. I have a lot of former cab drivers here and some of these boys and some of my farm boys too have mastered tank driving in 20 minutes. The ordinary course is 50 hours. The boy who has been driving a cab, or operating a tractor on a farm, he's the one who's become a glorious soldier for the tank unit."

America During Wartime Was—

America during wartime was a family of four with the son in the armed forces, the father in civilian defense, the mother in a war job, and the daughter in volunteer service. It was a female bellhop in the Hotel Alex Johnson in Rapid City, South Dakota, reading Ernie Pyle's *Brave Men* while "You'd Be So Nice to Come Home To" played in the cocktail bar. And it was a teenage mechanic at the Star Vulcanizing Works on San Antonio Street in El Paso (just around the corner from the Hotel Paso Del Norte) with his well-worn copy of Bill Mauldin's *Up Front*. It was a navy lieutenant junior grade from Wisconsin seeing the ocean for the first time from the mobbed boardwalk at Coney Island.

America during wartime was newspapers printing special calendars to explain the complicated rationing system:

> *Tomorrow—coffee coupon No. 25 expires. Last day to use No. 4 "A" coupon, good for four gallons of gasoline.*
>
> *March 25—processed food stamps for April, D, E, and F in Ration Book No. 2 becomes valid. The monthly quota of 48 points remains unchanged. Budget these through April 30.*

It was Americans learning not to ask for new cars, dishwashers, phonographs, lawn mowers, toasters, typewriters, refrigerators, radios—or thumbtacks or paper clips—and no new toothpaste unless you turned in your old tube. It was learning to do without.

America during wartime was the graveyard shift—workers by the hundreds of thousands working from midnight to 8 AM. It was an incredible crush at railroad stations, just as crowded in the the middle of the night as during rush hour.

In the wee hours of the morning at the State Bar Cafe on Main Street in Yuma, Arizona, a friendly crowd buzzed around the bar. Soldiers mixed with cowpunchers, hard-rock miners, truck drivers, and lettuce-packers. The great mirror behind the bar had been frosted over with Epsom salts and stale beer, and printed in varicolored lettering was:

V FOR AMERICA!
TO HELL WITH HITLER!
SLAP THE JAPS OFF THE MAP!
REMEMBER PEARL HARBOR!!!

A CALL TO ARMS

Shortly after Pearl Harbor, Lem Ah Toy, a Chinese laundryman in Seattle, hung this sign on the door of his closed shop: "Gone to War. Closed Duration. Will clean shirts after clean Axis. Thank you."

The rush to enlist started Monday, December 8, the morning after Pearl Harbor. By 7 AM there were 300 men standing in line at the Midtown Manhattan Army Recruiting Center. Total enlistments for the day were three times as great as on April 6, 1917, the first day of World War I. By the middle of the afternoon the marines had processed 500 men, the navy 700; the navy turned 1000 men away because there were not enough doctors to examine them.

There was an intoxicating blend of exhilaration and pride that came when loved ones enlisted. One woman remembers the intense and conflicting emotions almost everyone was feeling:

In the first week of May (1942) we got a letter from Aunt Mary saying that cousin Tommy had joined the Marines about a month earlier. She enclosed a snapshot of Tommy in his uniform fooling around with a cigarette holder in his mouth. I remember that we got the letter during the Battle of the Coral Sea. I was on the graveyard shift at the plant. We would take a break around 3:30. I would re-read the letter and every time I looked at the picture I would go through a roller coaster of emotions—very proud, yet terribly afraid...And the Coral Sea was simultaneously so sad and yet wonderful. We lost more ships than the Japanese and one of our carriers was destroyed.

I can remember Helena Bartone standing in the doorway holding our coffee and softly saying, "It was the Lexington." Just knowing the name of the ship made it more real. It was the first time I remember hearing the phrase, "major Allied victory." Those three words made me feel Tommy might be all right.

Celebrities were most visible, but people from all walks of life did their part for the war effort. Judy Garland (opposite) entertained workers at the Philadelphia Navy Yard. Above, Don Wilson and Edgar Kennedy help Betty Grable auction off her silk stockings at a war bond drive in Long Beach, California. Shut-ins sold bonds by telephone, and (below) the most successful salesman was congratulated by celebrities like (from left) Harpo Marx, Jimmy Cagney, Mickey Rooney, and Lucille Ball. Right, Warner Brothers drafted its cartoon characters as well. Bugs tells Joan Leslie, star of *Rhapsody in Blue*, he's going to put his "Easter eggs" where they'll do the most good.

Schoolkids from all over the country (above, in New York) scoured alleyways and empty lots for tin cans and other scrap metal. Ration books (right)—and the complicated rules for their use—became a part of the daily routine. So many motorists gassed up as soon as the news of Pearl Harbor came over the radio that they created a shortage that lasted for months.

Left, Frank Sinatra collects "scrap records for our fighting men" in midtown New York. (The effort was later dropped, as the reclamation process proved too costly.) Inset, above, some merchants made their own rules to aid the war effort Top, street-corner booths sold war stamps that could be converted to war bonds.

Victory gardens sprang up in empty lots everywhere. At right, women can the produce from a neighborhood garden. In the inset, below, children tend their own vegetable beds. Displays on behalf of war bonds, like the one below in Philadelphia, had the added benefit of boosting morale. The "Junior Treasury Commandos" on the float are urging onlookers to help contain Hirohito the snake, Hitler the rat, and Mussolini the skunk, represented by the animals in their cages.

At right, a "defense apron" that was supposed to be worn over the dresses of women working in defense plants. Practicality prevailed over "proper" dress, however, and most women donned slacks instead. At far right, a Victory Volunteer knits during a break at work. Idleness of any kind was deemed unpatriotic during the war years.

THIS IS A V HOME

if you talk too much

THIS MAN MAY DIE

Almost every home advertised its war contribution in a window. Most honored were homes displaying service flags or stars (right) indicating how many members of the household were in the services. Homes deemed worthy by local air wardens "for conservation, salvage, refusal to spread war rumors, and purchase of war bonds and stamps" were allowed to display Office of Civilian Defense (OCD) stickers in the window (top, left). Posters promoting vigilance against loose talk (left) and urging the purchase of war bonds (below) were seen everywhere.

BUY THAT INVASION BOND!

THE SEND-OFF

s America said goodbye to its fighting men, poignant scenes of farewell became familiar sights all across the nation. An 18-year-old who enlisted in the Army Air Forces recalls:

My mother was crushed and couldn't go down to Penn Station to see me off. My father and Paulie Ragusa were going. After a tearful goodbye, we left the apartment and started up 73rd Street. My father stopped, hugged me and sobbed, "I can't go to the train. I have to check on your mother." I agreed and hugged him back. He pressed a couple of dollars in Paulie's hand and said, "Grab a cab!" I wiped my eyes and said to Paulie, "Let's go."

And the wife of a major who was to command a bomber squadron remembers:

I remember very clearly the night they left Spokane—New Year's 1942. We had gotten in at dawn after a dance at the Officers' Club at Fort George Wright. We had slept very late. Felix got his orders that afternoon. He was to pick up a crew and leave by train for Seattle at nine o'clock the same evening. He was to take command of a new B-17 and fly it to Tampa, Florida. This seemed a backward sort of way to get to the Philippines.

We drove around and picked up his laundry and other belongings, then went back to the hotel for dinner. We had always had a good time in the Italian Gardens Room; we would dine once more and dance once more there together.

The white fluted pillars, with their wreaths of little colored lights; the cool dark plants in tubs, the orchestra playing "Blues in the Night" and "Elmer's Tune" and the Tchaikovsky Prelude that was popular then...the people in evening clothes....It could have been any Saturday night.

I thought, nobody seems sad. We talked about trivial things and ate our dinners. We danced and drank champagne. I knew that one was supposed to send soldiers away with a smile; I felt silly with tears trickling down my face.

At right, Staff Sgt. Robert Shackleton draws the first number for the second draft lottery. Because of grumblings about the fairness of the system, an enlisted man replaced Secretary of the Navy Frank Knox, who was to draw the number. At the sergeant's left is Charles Morris, who had picked the first number in the 1917 draft lottery.

Camp Stoneman, California, left, was the first stop for many soldiers on their way to the battlefields of the Pacific. Every day 4,500 men were processed there. Posters like the one below urged recruits to set aside differences for the sake of victory.

Volunteers often marched to the recruiting center, carrying banners and flanked by recruiters. Below, volunteers march to the enlistment center in Richmond, Virginia, six weeks before Pearl Harbor.

FIGHTING SIDE BY SIDE

PROTESTANT
CATHOLIC
JEW

©1944 INSTITUTE FOR AMERICAN DEMOCRACY INC.

So that Every Person may Worship God in his own way!

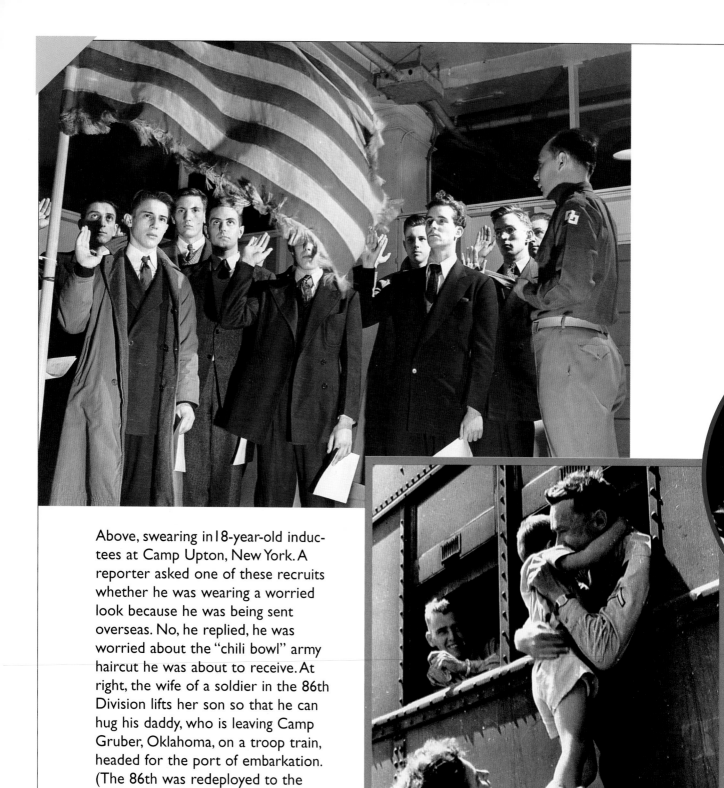

Above, swearing in 18-year-old induc-
tees at Camp Upton, New York. A
reporter asked one of these recruits
whether he was wearing a worried
look because he was being sent
overseas. No, he replied, he was
worried about the "chili bowl" army
haircut he was about to receive. At
right, the wife of a soldier in the 86th
Division lifts her son so that he can
hug his daddy, who is leaving Camp
Gruber, Oklahoma, on a troop train,
headed for the port of embarkation.
(The 86th was redeployed to the
Pacific after having seen combat in
Europe.)

Below, a woman parting with her boy-friend as he leaves Boston for naval aviation training in Chapel Hill, North Carolina, crosses her fingers in hopes that he will return safely. The woman at right gets a good-bye kiss with the help of her soldier's friends. Bottom, soldiers boarding a Pacific-bound troop transport.

The United Service Organizations (USO) centers were sponsored by church and civic organizations to provide a wholesome place where soldiers could meet their families or spend off-duty time. The USO also provided shows that traveled to bases. Above, the cast of one show, *Razzle, Dazzle,* gets a send-off at New York's Penn Station in December 1941.

You help someone you know...

when you give to

the USO

HOWARD SCOTT

The Stage Door Canteen, sponsored by the American Theater Wing, opened in 1942 in a basement on Broadway and 44th Street. Soldiers came by the hundreds to rub shoulders with actors and actresses. Seven other Stage Door Canteens were opened by the USO around the country, but the original one in New York (left) was the one best remembered.

Alvin Josephy

Before the war Alvin Josephy had reported on the realities of the Depression for the Mutual Broadcasting System. He served as a Marine Corps combat correspondent on Guam and Iwo Jima. When he returned, he became a Hollywood screenwriter, a reporter for *Time*, and then an editor for *American Heritage*.

Because he worked at a radio station, Josephy heard about the bombing of Pearl Harbor before most of the country got the news.

I was listening to another station playing music, classical music, and shaving, I had a towel around me. I lived down in Greenwich Village at the time. The phone rang and—we had only one or two people up in master control at WOR—and one of them said that the ticker tape came in that we were being attacked at Pearl Harbor. So I switched to our station right away and we were broadcasting a football game. Finally we got word to an announcer or somebody and the public address system at the stadium ordered all members of the navy to report back to their ships right away and army people to leave and go back to their stations. And that was the first word any of us got of what was going on.

Although he spent much of his life in journalism, it was Josephy's experience as a marine in World War II that had the greatest impact on his life:

It's my belief that practically every combat veteran of World War II looks back on his war experience as the greatest experience in his life. And, nothing can top it; he goes to his grave with that memory as being his greatest moment. Now you take the fellow who had been mowing your lawn, and then suddenly he's out in the Pacific, being landed in the darkness of night on a Japanese-held island from a submarine and supposed to stay on that island, out of sight of the Japanese—maybe all by himself, maybe with a little team—until they take him off three nights later, when he's got to signal to a submarine offshore. That's the biggest thing in that man's life. Then he went back home and mowed lawns again.

Josephy reflected on the difficulty he and many other war veterans experienced integrating into life back home.

Many veterans were unable or unwilling to talk about combat or anything they had been through with anybody back home. They'd do it among themselves...in the veterans' halls in a more joshing way. They'd say, "Hey, you remember so-and-so...." And instead of remembering something terrible about him, they'd remember something good or funny. But you never wanted to talk to your family or anybody who hadn't been there. And I think it was because of a deep psychological feeling of guilt that you had come through and...and Andy hadn't.

THE REALITY OF WAR

Pearl Harbor taught Americans that they should expect anything. In the first two years of the war, people in California, Oregon, and Washington considered themselves to be in "the Pacific Front Line." Attack from Japan was a realistic possibility. Major William Devin of Seattle told a reporter:

Seattle is the number one target in the entire US. Our city is within bombing distance of Kiska and Attu islands. The Japs are currently completing airfields on these [Aleutian] islands.

A leading Seattle businessman had this to say:

Do we expect a bombing? Why, of course we do. We're the closest to Alaska, and therefore the closest important port to Japan. We're accessible by waterways from Japanese territory. We're on Puget Sound and you simply can't black out a body of water like that. Many of us feel that the Japs will come at us from the north, that it won't take any great efforts to slip submarines into Puget Sound.

In San Francisco too, an assault was anticipated. Mayor Angelo J. Rossi spoke to a reporter from New York:

We have 635,000 people in San Francisco and not one will run. Sooner or later we all think we're going to hear from the Japs. We bombed Tokyo, didn't we? Well, the Japs won't forget that. Tell the people in New York that out here we all feel that some day we'll see little strangers in the skies and we'll give them a hot reception.

On the East Coast, Nazi submarines sank ships within sight of land. Along the Atlantic, coastal dwellers became accustomed to sudden, brilliant flashes of explosions light-

How news of the war reached America: wireless operators used high-speed encoders to send 400 words per minute round the clock to relay stations in Hawaii.

ing up the night sky. Afterwards, bodies washed ashore, along with charred life boats, fragments of life jackets, and dead fish. Residents feared that the Germans would launch small planes from U-boats to bomb them.

One Long Island woman remembered what many people were thinking:

They had just posted a new casualty list, and Joanie and Graham had found a body on the beach. Bataan and Corrigedor had fallen. I remember looking out at lilacs from the kitchen window thinking 'spring' but feeling weary and disheartened, unsure of everything, wondering when the war was coming.

The bombing in daylight of the power station at Knapsack, Germany, by the Royal Air Force.

BACK THEM UP!

The early days of the war forced America to look into the face of defeat for the first time in its history. Ten hours after Pearl Harbor, the Japanese launched a second surprise attack, this time against Gen. Douglas MacArthur's air base in the Philippines. Half the US aircraft in the South Pacific were wiped out. Then Guam, Wake Island, Hong Kong, Borneo, the Dutch East Indies, Bataan, and Corregidor all fell. Photos of the Bataan Death March (top) were not published until 1945, but the story was widely known thanks to correspondent John Hersey's reports. As many as 10,000 men died on the march. Despite the loss of the Philippines, MacArthur (right) was still considered a brilliant military leader, thanks largely to Hersey's book, *Men on Bataan*.

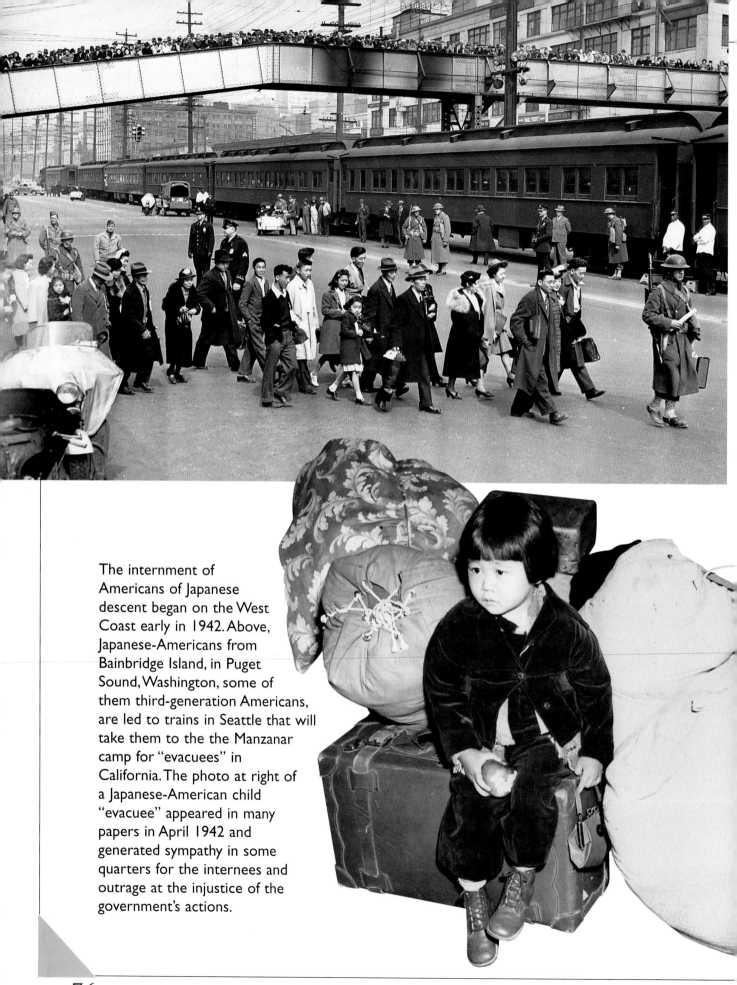

The internment of Americans of Japanese descent began on the West Coast early in 1942. Above, Japanese-Americans from Bainbridge Island, in Puget Sound, Washington, some of them third-generation Americans, are led to trains in Seattle that will take them to the the Manzanar camp for "evacuees" in California. The photo at right of a Japanese-American child "evacuee" appeared in many papers in April 1942 and generated sympathy in some quarters for the internees and outrage at the injustice of the government's actions.

The anti-Japanese hysteria that followed Pearl Harbor was long-lasting and pervasive. Non-Japanese workers of Far Eastern descent in defense plants wore signs like the one at right as late as 1948. The racist sign below was in a Boston restaurant in late 1941. The barbershop sign, bottom, appeared throughout Kent, Washington, when rumors spread that Japanese internees would be allowed to return to their homes after the war.

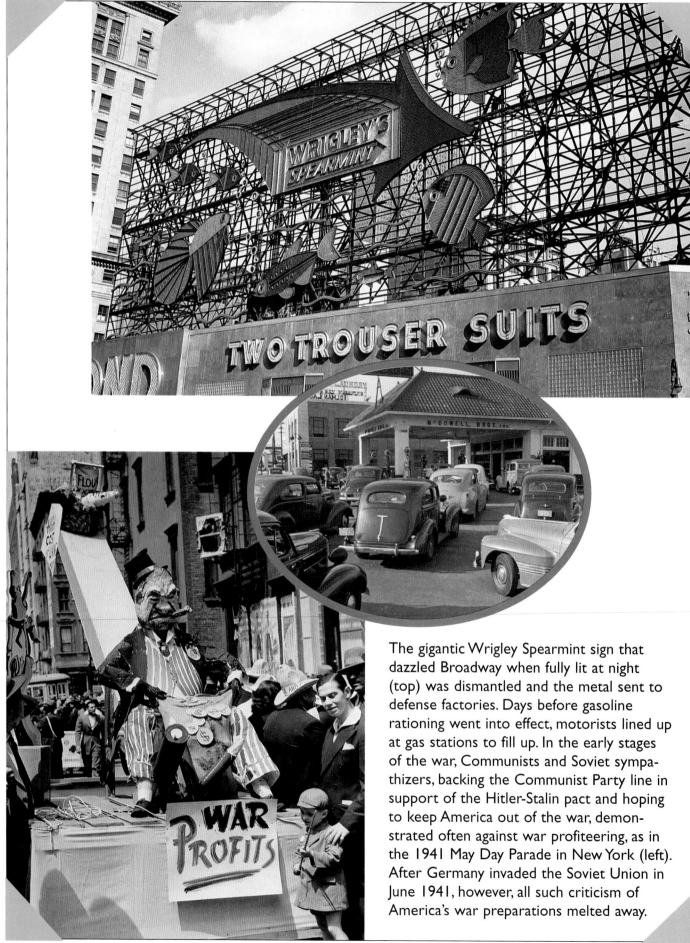

The gigantic Wrigley Spearmint sign that dazzled Broadway when fully lit at night (top) was dismantled and the metal sent to defense factories. Days before gasoline rationing went into effect, motorists lined up at gas stations to fill up. In the early stages of the war, Communists and Soviet sympathizers, backing the Communist Party line in support of the Hitler-Stalin pact and hoping to keep America out of the war, demonstrated often against war profiteering, as in the 1941 May Day Parade in New York (left). After Germany invaded the Soviet Union in June 1941, however, all such criticism of America's war preparations melted away.

Valentine Miele & Frederick Erben

Valentine Miele of Jersey City and Frederick Erben (right) of Brooklyn were members of the 16th Infantry Regiment, 1st Division, which first saw combat in North Africa during World War II. They recalled their experiences at a VFW hall in Lindenhurst, New York.

Miele: *I can remember when I got hit. I got blown up in the air. I laid out there all day and all night before they picked me up. Then when they picked me up, the grave diggers came over by me. And I said, "Hey, over here! Hey, hey!" The guy said, "Hey, we got a live one." And they picked me up and they carried me out. This bone here was way over here. Piece of shrapnel over there. Blood stopped right away with the mud. And I laid there all day and all night—I was there a solid twenty-four hours. My feet turned black. It was January.*

The experiences of the war created a powerful bond between the men in C Company that remained strong over 50 years later.

Erben: *We were closer than anybody we ever grew up with. We were family. Well, this C Company is my family now.*

Miele: *My wife says to me, "Hey, you going to send Christmas cards?" "Yeah, I'm sending. I already sent mine out." "Who the hell did you send them to?" "I sent them to my family."*

The bond is so strong because, they believe, only a select few have shared the real horror of war.

Erben: *I was home and my sister wanted to go to a movie, so we went to a movie. It was a war picture. I got up and walked out. I just couldn't handle it. And I didn't realize how bad I felt until that particular moment. I says, "The movie don't tell the full story," really. Brought back too many memories. I walked out. My sister come out and we went home. I says, "I don't want to see nothing about war anymore." Nobody can understand what we went through.*

After returning home, Erben was mistaken for someone who hadn't served in the military.

I come home in the States, first time I put on civilian clothes. I bought them from Howard's Clothes, $29.95 for a suit. So I'm walking down the street, and one young lady says, "What are you doing over here? You should be over there with the service. You're 4-F?" I says, "Yeah, I am, honey." And I just walked by. She's yelling at me. I couldn't believe it. So somebody that I knew went over to the young lady and says, "You know, he just come back from the war." She was red-faced. The next day I see her walking down, she tried to apologize, I says, "Don't bother, lady."

ARSENAL OF DEMOCRACY

Posters like the one above and special pins (top) emphasized the importance of industry for success on the battlefield.

By midsummer 1942, American war production had reached the level it would maintain for the remainder of the conflict. Initially there had been inefficiency and waste, strikes and gripes, fumbling and grumbling, too much red tape, anger and frustration with inept regulation. The chaos was aptly described by a series of acronyms borrowed from the military: *snafu* (situation normal, all fouled up), *tarfu* (things are really fouled up), and *fubar* (fouled up beyond all recognition). But the kinks were worked out and the red tape overcome. The prodigious production effort succeeded beyond our wildest dreams. It was a monumental achievement the likes of which the world had never seen—or even suspected of being possible.

In San Diego, Tom Mercer Girdler, former steelman, spoke to a reporter about making bombers:

We're going along like fury and so is the entire aircraft industry. We're paying around 90 cents an hour, and our payroll is averaging around $7,500,000 monthly—for approximately 35,000 workers. You see, it costs money to build airplanes. And so many people want to work in the airplane factories. Why, I went into the barbershop at the El Cortez Hotel and the barber asked me for a job. The manicurist wanted to give up manicuring and come work at the plant.

A New Jerseyite remembered planes and tanks from the summer he was 12:

Phil and I would be having a catch, maybe just talking about the war, or maybe we'd taken out our spotter cards. There were two kinds. One kind was actual playing cards. I had International Aircraft Silhouettes, so you got all countries. Ace of diamonds was a German Focke-Wulf. Ace of hearts was a British bomber—Lancaster, I think. Ace of clubs: Japanese fighter Mitsubishi Type O, also known as Zeke. Ace of spades: U.S. bomber B-17E Flying Fortress. Big favorite. And I remember the Spitfire was the six of hearts. So we'd wait for the tank trains. And as soon as we caught the first glimpse, we'd run toward the tracks jumping and shouting, "Rommel Routers." There would be nothing but tanks. The whole train was flatcars with tanks. Sometimes we'd start to count them but we'd never finish. I couldn't believe there were so many tanks.

Women workers (left) were the mainstay of the assembly line building the B-24 Liberators in Fort Worth, Texas. Defense workers lived near the plants in government-supplied "V-trailers." These are some of the 2,000 trailers passing the Lincoln Memorial on their way to Wilmington, North Carolina. The task of clothing 500,000 new soldiers in four months was carried out in dozens of manufacturing lofts in the New York garment district (below). Union rallies, like this one in Madison Square Garden (below, left) were used to boost morale and address grievances.

At Grumman Aircraft's plant in Bethpage, Long Island (left), workers assemble rows of Wildcat fighter planes for the navy.

Aircraft manufacturers discovered that women workers put rivets in place with greater care than men. At right, thousands of clamps hold the fuselage of a C-54 Skymaster together before riveting. Below, an inspector at the navy's Alexandria, Virginia, torpedo plant measures the diameter of a torpedo casing, which must be accurate to within one ten-thousandth of an inch.

Artillery shells are marked with chalk before being tested at Fort Andrews near Boston. The practice of painting bombs came from the need to identify shrapnel on the test range. The custom was extended to marking all military equipment with phrases and drawings, creating in the process a new art form. Below, workers at the Douglas Long Beach, California, plant celebrate the completion of their 3,000th C-47 Skytrain as it rolls off the assembly line. The mark was reached in just 14 months of production.

At right, the first models of the M-4 tank come off the assembly line at the Pullman factory in Hammond, Indiana, in the summer of 1942. A year earlier, Pullman had been building railroad sleeping cars.

Dubbed "Liberty Ships," cargo vessels for the Merchant Marine were produced at California shipyards at the dizzying pace of a ship every two days through 1944, and at the impossible rate of a ship a day by the beginning of 1945.

Smokey Montgomery

Smokey Montgomery was a banjo player with a band called the Light Crust Doughboys. Born in 1913, he grew up on a farm in Iowa, a few miles from a town with a population of only 160.

The Doughboys, like other Americans, were required to put down their instruments and work for the war effort.

World War II was in the making and about 1941 they started rationing gasoline. We couldn't get tires for the bus, so they couldn't send us out on trips. And the guys—Cecil Broder went into the coast guard. Frank Reno went to the army. And the guys started getting drafted, or went into the service. We was having a hard time finding good musicians, and so in '42 they disbanded the Doughboys.

So right then we...we knew it. We was going to have to start going to the war. So I immediately took a refresher course, which the government paid for, in machine shop. And so I immediately got a job with a machine shop that was making shells for the navy, six-inch shells. And it's the only time I ever used any of my college education as a matter of fact. I wouldn't go through it again, but I wouldn'ta missed it.

The stark reality of American racism came as a shock to the Iowa banjo player.

And I learned a few things on that...that I hadn't thought much about, being from Iowa. I had some colored people working for me, and they cleaned out the machines and stuff. That's what you're supposed to do. And one night I was shorthanded and I put one of those fellows to running one of the machines. He could run any of them as good as anybody else. The next day we had a strike on our hands 'cause I put a black man running one of the machines that a white man had been running. And up to that time that part of what was going on never had hit me before. Being a musician, if you could play a guitar good—we didn't care what color—we'd go set in with 'em, they'd come set in with us. But when you got down to the real world like making shells for the navy, I realized that...that didn't work.

Does Smokey have any regrets?

I guess I've been the luckiest guy in the world, musician-wise. I've always been in the right place at the right time. I've always been able to do what I wanted to do....Even during World War II, I loved making those shells and trying to get the war over with.

And I'm still picking on the old banjo and still having fun. If I wasn't here tomorrow, I wouldn't mind, because I feel like my life's been so complete. And if I had to do the whole life over again, the only thing I'd do is pick a shorter name. I've had to sign that Marvin Montgomery so many times, I'd make it Joe P. or something like that.

THE WOMEN OF WWII

A photographer was recalling some of his favorite wartime work:

I'd done a series for Pan Am. One that I really liked was of three women mechanics who were giving the final check to propellers that had been serviced in the overhaul shop. You had the women standing. The one on the right was reaching up with her left hand. Part of each propeller was over them so you had this half-a-canopy effect with the light on the propellers and it didn't hurt that each girl was long-legged and beautiful.

Another favorite was of four girls who'd just been promoted to engineers working on an oil tank in the welding shop. Three wore safety glasses. The fourth had hers pushed back on her forehead. She was listening intently to the chief mechanic-instructor who was supervising. A close-up I liked a lot was of a girl mechanic lifting a 70-lb. blade to the hub of a propeller—they called them 'domes' —while the propeller-shop chief leans forward to make sure everything's all right. That girl couldn't have been over five feet but she had absolutely no trouble with that blade. I remember that.

A woman worker has vivid memories of the 11 PM to 7 AM graveyard shift at a defense plant:

I remember three things: One, that the Italians were happier and more talkative than everybody. Two, the birds were quieter. Three: you could always get a seat on the bus home because most everybody was going in the opposite direction. Italian prisoners of war worked in the dining hall. They served the food, washed dishes, mopped the floor. For some reason the ones on the grave-yard were a lot happier than the daytime ones. Maybe it was just a coincidence. I remember one of them asked me for a picture so I gave him one of me on the beach.

Birds used to come in through the ventilator and then they couldn't get out. During the day they'd actually land in your hair. But at night they'd calm down and just sort of stand around. And they weren't so skittish.

I remember Nan O'Neill would stand maybe five or six feet away and would talk to them. I can see her in coveralls holding her coffee saying, "What's with you guys? How come you're not flying around? When I'm here at 2 PM you're going crazy, swooping all over the place." She was really great.

Women MPs (opposite) usually got better cooperation from soldiers than men MPs did. Left, the WACs recruited heavily throughout the war and offered generous benefits. Below, a WAC corporal with the crew of the Liberator bomber, the *G.I. Jane*, sporting the insignia of Pallas Athene, symbol of the WAC. Bottom, army nurses formed softball teams and toured bases, paving the way for the creation of a professional all-woman baseball league. In the background, WAVE machinists at the training center in Norman, Oklahoma, stay fit with regular calisthenics.

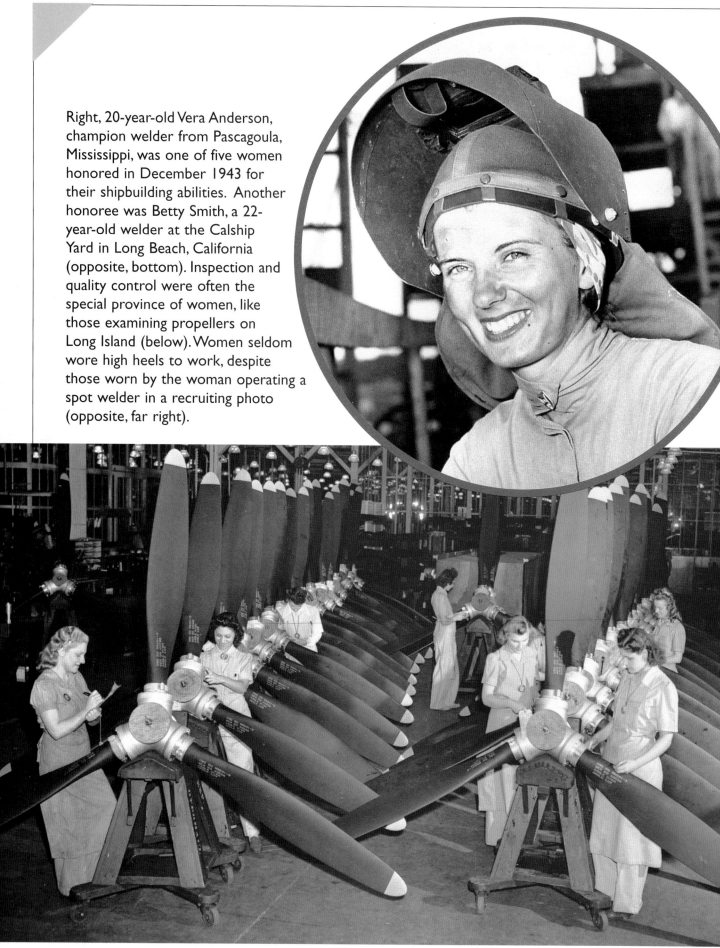

Right, 20-year-old Vera Anderson, champion welder from Pascagoula, Mississippi, was one of five women honored in December 1943 for their shipbuilding abilities. Another honoree was Betty Smith, a 22-year-old welder at the Calship Yard in Long Beach, California (opposite, bottom). Inspection and quality control were often the special province of women, like those examining propellers on Long Island (below). Women seldom wore high heels to work, despite those worn by the woman operating a spot welder in a recruiting photo (opposite, far right).

We Can Do It!

Hundreds of hardworking patriotic women proudly bore the sobriquet Rosie the Riveter. J. Howard Miller based his "Rosie the Riveter" poster (above) on Rose Monroe, a worker in the Willow Run aircraft plant in Ypsilanti, Michigan. The actor Walter Pidgeon visited the plant and included Monroe in a promotional film for war bonds. The inspiration for the Kay Kyser band's hit recording "Rosie the Riveter" was a Long Island woman who worked in an aircraft plant.

Doris Day sings to the accompaniment of the Les Brown Orchestra in 1941 (left). In spite of her high exposure, Day was strictly a secondary part of the act in the days before the war. The status of women in the United States was greatly enhanced by First Lady Eleanor Roosevelt, below, delivering her memorable address the night of Pearl Harbor.

Riding a wave of interest in Latin America, dancer Carmen Miranda (left) reached the height of her fame during the war years. Her trademark was sky-scraping hats, often laden with fresh fruit. The Andrews Sisters (right, in 1944) were among the first female singers to take top billing over a male-led orchestra.

Left, Hollywood gossip columnist Hedda Hopper (wearing one of her trademark hats) christens a Douglas C-47 ambulance plane named after her. Hopper's radio broadcasts were beamed overseas to give GIs the latest on their favorite movie stars. Below, an American institution by the early 1940s, Kate Smith became a symbol of home to young soldiers. Her shows were highlighted by her rendition of the Irving Berlin classic "God Bless America," for which she purchased the exclusive radio rights in 1938.

By the 1940s the Fuller Brush Man was an American institution. But in 1942, the manpower shortage was becoming severe, and the first Fuller Brush Woman, Louise Morgan, began making her rounds in Cleveland. Meanwhile, the early computers had a woman at the controls. Below, Lt. Grace Hopper, inventor of the programming language that computers used to calculate artillery ranges. Bottom, the nerve center of the War Production Board, housed in an old skating rink (note the pads around the pillars) in downtown Washington, gave enormous discretionary authority to office workers, nearly all of whom were women, to interpret the new regulations.

Peggy Terry

Peggy Terry grew up in an impoverished coal-miner family in Kentucky. During the war she left her home and found work in a munitions factory.

Terry saw the war change American values, creating new opportunities for women.

The notion that you may die tomorrow, you know, it was the kind of thing that just permeated the whole population... you know, the boys going off to England and being bombed and all that. But things that wouldn't have been tolerated before, it was suddenly okay.

Like women going into bars. There wasn't a bar in Paducah where a woman was allowed, and then when the war came we were allowed to go in. I always wanted to go in the Palmer Bar because it was so beautiful. The bar was a half a block long and had a brass rail, brass spittoons. I had always wanted to see it. And that was one proud day when my sister and my girlfriend and I went into the Palmer Bar and sat down and had a beer.

Although women laborers were essential during the war, Terry's male coworkers made it difficult for her and other women in the munitions plant.

Oh, they'd make nasty remarks. This sex...well, what you would call harassment today, you know, sexual harassment. And they always criticized your work. Like the guy that worked on the machine next to me,

he hated me. He used to tell me every day...why don't you go home and take care of your children? And he...he would complain to my foreman that I was getting so many rejects and he got sick of it. All that foreman cared about was if you did good work. And my work was good. I had fewer rejects than this guy did. So he told him, if you don't like it, you can move back out in the shop, you know, out of calibration. So then he really did hate me. And he used to put tape on my chair and when I'd sit down...it'd stick to my clothing....He was a real creep.

Terry realized that although her life was significantly improved due to the war, the better life at home came at the expense of those fighting overseas.

Well, you know, everybody in this country benefited from that war...but our boys were over there paying for it...All they talk about is the glory of going. Well, if they could see some of the things that I saw. My sister and I worked in this army hospital in Killeen, Texas, right down close to Waco. And they had this one really wonderful guy, he got the bottom part of his face shot away ...and he told us to call him "the chinless wonder."

I got mail from him for a long time. Not love letters, just friends. He was such a...a wonderful guy. So many of them were— young guys. God, your heart would just break every day.

FDR IN AMERICA'S CONSCIOUSNESS

In early 1942, just six weeks after Pearl Harbor, the staunchly isolationist Chicago *Tribune* (published by anti-New Dealer Col. Robert R. McCormick) wrote: "Our president is removable only by the long process of impeachment." Shortly thereafter the New York *Daily News* warned: "This administration expects to be running some sort of totalitarian government either before or after the end of the war." Out on the fringe, Elizabeth Dilling, in her *Patriotic Research Bureau Newsletter*, dubbed FDR the "Stooge of the International Socialist-Communist Collectivist Judaistic World Government."

Yet the overwhelming majority of Americans not only approved of the job the president was doing, they felt genuine affection for him. His reassuring voice on the radio and his twinkle-in-the-eye and silently mischievous smile (often

with the trademark cigarette holder thrust jauntily upward) had come to represent a modern, quintessentially American blend of optimism, courage, decency, and good will. While FDR was in office, you could find citizens of every walk of life proudly displaying a picture of their president.

One reporter spent an evening in San Francisco's Chinatown asking people how they felt about the war:

I finished my punch made of Peruvian brandy, bade good night to Chingwah Lee, wandered back to California Street, and boarded a clanking cable car, bound for Nob Hill. Taking stock of this Chinatown evening, I'd seen six photographs of Roosevelt along the way.

It was much the same for a Kansas City resident: *My Uncle Mac (his real name was McKinley) owned a barbershop. By the cash register he had a photo of his son in his uniform, some clippings about his outfit, some other family photos, a Monarchs team pennant from the Negro League, his first dollar— stuff like that. But on the wall above the chairs—not the barber chairs, but the chairs where you sat and waited—he had only one picture: President Roosevelt. We'd kid him, "Why don't you put Joe Louis up or Jimmie Lunceford?" He'd say, "No sir. That wall is only for the president."*

And in a quite different setting: *All my uncles and six cousins, they all worked on the docks. They called them the Pistol Locals. Albert Anastasia, his brother, Tough Tony, Dandy Jack Parisi—you get the idea. Anyway, there was only one picture hanging in the whole place, and it wasn't Tough Tony. And it sure wasn't LaGuardia. It was President Roosevelt. And they kept it clean.*

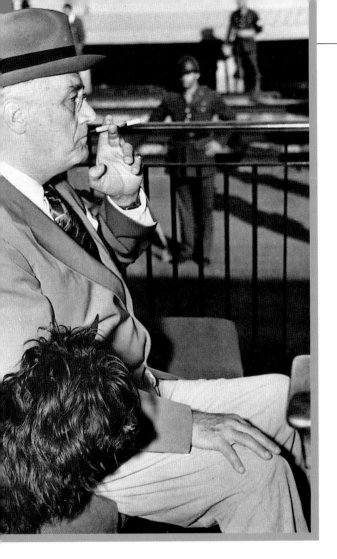

FDR seated with his dog, Fala, on the rear platform of his special train in 1943 (left). Roosevelt used the medium of radio (opposite, a 1938 fireside chat broadcast) to great effect, not only to persuade, but to illuminate. Newspapers published maps (below) that the president would use during his address to illustrate his point.

Below, left, signature symbols of FDR: His cigarette holder and the V-for-Victory sign. Roosevelt was adept at projecting an image of vitality, though he was stricken with polio and could not walk unaided. There are nearly no photographs extant that show him using crutches or seated in a wheelchair, and only one brief film clip of him being supported as he walked.

I WANT YOU F.D.R.

STAY AND FINISH THE JOB!

INDEPENDENT VOTERS' COMMITTEE OF THE
ARTS and SCIENCES for ROOSEVELT

The avuncular image of Roosevelt contrasted sharply with the image that world leaders had always presented in photographs and posters. Yet FDR did not try to hide his aristocratic upbringing; it actually helped him deal with potentates, such as Saudi King Ibn Saud, shown below with Roosevelt at a 1945 meeting.

FDR knew how to use the press to influence public opinion and as an extension of the office of the presidency. He often offered suggestions for headlines and stories (left), which editors were usually eager to accept. Below, his wife, Eleanor, helped keep FDR abreast of public sentiment.

"USO deserves the support of every individual citizen"

Franklin D Roosevelt

GIVE TO USO

General Outdoor Adv. Co.

The use of the president's image in supporting the USO, a private, nongovernmental enterprise, was unusual at the time, but FDR knew when his backing was needed. President Roosevelt's sudden death in April 1945, five months after his election for an unprecedented fourth term, left the nation in a state of shock (below). Thousands of mourners, below right, lined the route of the funeral procession. Inset shows the cortege approaching the Capitol.

"WE'LL ALWAYS HAVE PARIS"

In December 1941, the president made the following statement: *The American motion picture is one of our most effective mediums in informing and entertaining our citizens. The motion picture must remain free insofar as national security will permit. I want no censorship of the motion picture.*

Hollywood did succeed admirably in bringing every aspect of the war home to American audiences. Whether it was nurses on Bataan, Nazis in Canada, Philippine insurgents, or spies in Morocco or Istanbul, the movies emphasized that it truly was a global conflict that Americans were engaged in. Jingoistic excesses were to be expected. After all, it was wartime. Stakes were unbelievably high. Millions of people were dying. Among other things, this meant the Golden Age of Hollywood one-dimensional villainy. Actors like Conrad Veidt (a Jew who fled the Nazis) and Cedric Hardwicke (British) became the perfect embodiment of cold-hearted, Third Reich ruthlessness as they repeatedly delivered lines like "It is our destiny to conquer" and "There is no room for sentimentality in the new order."

Chinese-American actor Sen Yung found himself busily alternating between comedy and villainy. One month he would play Charlie Chan's impetuous, fumbling but lovable number one son, Jimmy. The next month he would become the oily personification of the sneering, treacherous Jap (usually educated in the United States, giving him a wide-ranging command of American slang). Then it would be back to broad comedy for another Chan mystery.

George Sanders alternated too. His chilly suavity was perfect for Nazi arrogance, but by adding a dash of poise and cheeky confidence, he became a stalwart British ally. Peter Lorre was in a class by himself. He was probably the only actor in Hollywood who could play both Japanese and Nazis, as well as any number of allied nationalities. As a heartless Nipponese spy, he got to say: "The Rising Sun never sets, so its spies never sleep." Then in the next film he played a tough French criminal with a strong love of country, ready to die for a free France.

Along the way, Hollywood managed to turn out some inspiring movies—*Air Force*, *They Were Expendable*, *Sahara*, *Mrs. Miniver*, *Across the Pacific*. And there was that superb example of just how good Hollywood wartime movies could be: Humphrey Bogart and Ingrid Bergman in *Casablanca*.

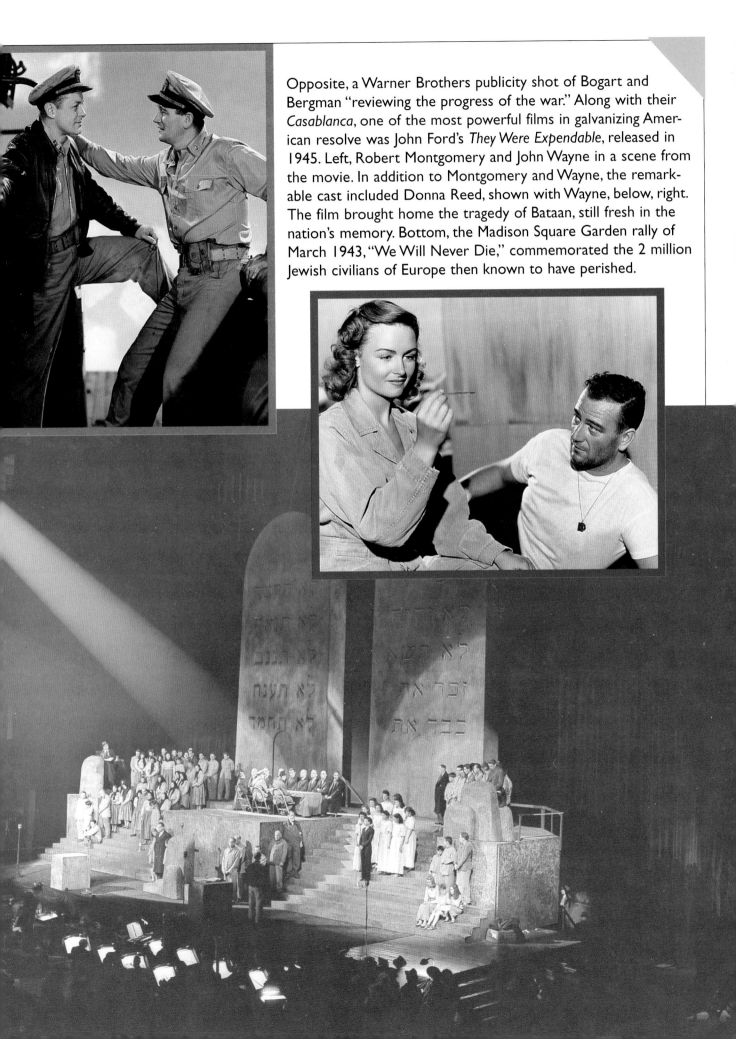

Opposite, a Warner Brothers publicity shot of Bogart and Bergman "reviewing the progress of the war." Along with their *Casablanca*, one of the most powerful films in galvanizing American resolve was John Ford's *They Were Expendable*, released in 1945. Left, Robert Montgomery and John Wayne in a scene from the movie. In addition to Montgomery and Wayne, the remarkable cast included Donna Reed, shown with Wayne, below, right. The film brought home the tragedy of Bataan, still fresh in the nation's memory. Bottom, the Madison Square Garden rally of March 1943, "We Will Never Die," commemorated the 2 million Jewish civilians of Europe then known to have perished.

During the days after Pearl Harbor, news was gathered in such volume that the Times Square news ticker (below) went weeks without repeating a headline. Bottom, Don Senick, one of the principal photographers in the Pacific for Movietone News, aims his specially rigged camera like a rifle.

War reporting made reputations. Shown above at left is Walter Cronkite, then of the United Press.

Ernie Pyle (above) and Margaret Bourke-White (right) were already highly respected—he as a journalist; she as a news photographer—when they brought their considerable talents to documenting the war. Pyle was killed while covering the fighting on Ie Shima in April 1945.

TRANS-LUX PRESENTS A SPECIAL V-J DAY PROGRAM

Timescope

Arsenal of Democracy

In 1941 FDR called upon American Industry to build 50,000 aircraft per year.

U.S. Aircraft Production, WWII

1942	47,000
1943	86,000
1944	103,000

Total aircraft built, 1941 to 1945: 296,429

War Production, 1941-1945

Small Arms	41,585,000	rounds
Aerial Bombs	5,822	tons
Trucks	2.456	million
Naval Ships	71,062	
Cargo Ships	5,425	
Artillery Guns	372,431	
Tanks	102,341	

America at War

U.S. Military Personnel (Active)

1918	2,897,167
1940	**458,365**
1941	**1,801,101**
1942	**3,858,791**
1943	**9,044,745**
1944	**11,451,719**
1945	**12,123,455**
1946	**3,030,088**
1949	**1,460,261**
1966	3,095,058
1988	2,128,000

U.S. Military Casualties (Deaths/Wounded)

World War I	116,516 / 204,002
World War II	**405,399 / 670,846**
Korean War	33,746 / 103,284
Vietnam War	58,151 / 153,303

The Funny Papers

Ten Most Popular Comic Strips of World War

1. Joe Palooka
2. Blondie
3. L'il Abner
4. Little Orphan Annie
5. Terry and the Pirates
6. Dick Tracy
7. Moon Mullins
8. Gasoline Alley
9. Bringing Up Father
10. The Gumps

Night on the Town

Prices of the "best seat in the house," 1945

Ice Show	$1.00
(New York) City	
Center Concert	$2.40
Broadway Show	$3.00
Ballet International	$3.50
Arthur Rubenstein in Concert,	
Carnegie Hall	$3.60

Three-course Dinner
(with glass of champagne)
at New York's Copacabana: $2.50

A Night at the Movies

Average Price of a Move Ticket / Total Number of Moviegoers

	$0.24 / 3.90 million
1935	$0.24 / 4.16
1940	$0.35 / 4.68
1945	$0.53 / 3.12
1950	$0.50 / 3.39
1955	$5.03 / 1.15
1990	

Box Office Receipts, in $ million / (Adjusted to 1987 dollars)

	$566 / ($4,693 million)
1935	$735 / ($5,964)
1940	$1,450 / ($9,151)
1945	$1,376 / ($6,486)
1950	$1,326 / ($5,620)
1955	$5,200 / ($4,722)
1990	

Strange Fact of 1945

On April 13, 1945, The New York Times reported that in the hour following the death of FDR (from 4:00 to 5:00 PM April 12), its switchboard had received 10,500 calls (a record for a single hour) reporting rumors of the death of the following celebrities:

1. Jack Dempsey	2,140	calls
2. Errol Flynn	1,310	
3. Babe Ruth	1,162	
4. Charlie Chaplin	914	
5. Frank Sinatra	785	
6. Jack Benny	730	
7. Jimmy Walker	529	
8. Gov. Herbert Lehman	317	
9. Harry Hopkins	284	

The text written on the train car:

MOVE OVER GOD IT'S MAC

32nd

STICK WITH MAC AND YOU'LL NEVER GET BACK

I HAVE GO

WERE THE BOYS WHO DUG OUT "DOUG" WHY PHILIPPINE C

("ADVANCE AUSTRALIA FAIR")

THRU THESE DOORS WILL PASS MEN WHO WILL BE LOOKING FOR → YOU KNOW WHAT

41 ST

They came home (above) after fighting two wars against two formidable enemies—both of them well-armed and hell-bent—on opposite sides of the globe. It had been a long, destructive, and costly war. And it finally came to a close in the Pacific after two A-bombs were dropped on the Japanese homeland (at right, the atomic blast at Nagasaki). Like many of the servicemen who had fought the war, America, and indeed the whole world, had changed for good.

V-J Day. The defeat of Japan triggered one of the greatest celebrations the country had ever seen. The end of the war brought nationwide euphoria—jubilation, exultation. Church bells rang out across the land. Factory whistles blew. Ship foghorns bellowed and car horns blared. There were impromptu pedestrian parades everywhere. There was dancing in the streets; snakelike conga lines were the favorites. Strangers embraced and kissed. There were huge bonfires, firecrackers, and lots of confetti. A million-plus people jammed into Times Square, and a dozen Eskimos in Barrow, Alaska, did a victory dance and banged drums made of walrus skin and driftwood. And accompanying the boisterous festivities were sober reflection and prayerful thanksgiving. Throughout the nation, churches and synagogues kept their doors open around the clock. Special services were packed. The United States of America breathed a deep, collective sigh of relief: "It's over."

Home for Christmas

The most popular words in the last half of 1945 were "home for Christmas." Trains and buses were packed with returning servicemen. It was a time of happy telegrams:

Arrived in New York last night. Will be home as soon as possible; will wire again from Denver and let you know details. Love to everyone.—Charles.

Arrived Bradley Field late last night. Almost called but knew all would be asleep. Only three train rides to go. Can't wait. With all my love.—Paul.

And joyful letters:

I'd been either too excited to sleep or too sleepy to be excited, but when I finally got to Union Station, it really hit me. I saw the flags of every allied nation hanging and, of course, I thought of all those times with Aunt Sue and Uncle Joe, Michael and Little Juney (remember how Otto used to pick her up and she would say Chicago, Milwaukee, St. Paul, and Pacific—and he used to play poker in the brakeman's

CHANGING TIMES
The Modern Era Begins

locker room?) I saw all the familiar signs: Shine 10 cents. Hats cleaned...and with each one I told myself, "You're home. You're Home. You're home."

Europe in Ruins

An ocean away, the story was quite different. At war's end, Europe lay totally ravaged. The Germans referred to their own country as being at *die stunde null*—hour zero. The same could be said the entire continent. One observer described Germany thus: *A land of ruins peopled by ghosts, without government, order or purpose, without industry, communications or the proper means of existence.... It had sunk to a level unknown in the Western world.*

Another, writing of trying to locate prewar friends in Cologne, reported: *Not a soul was in sight and not a sound was to be heard....There is a silence over everything. People whisper as if they are afraid to wake the dead below the debris. This is a cemetery and one does not make any noise in a cemetery.*

And a third correspondent, reporting from Duesseldorf, wrote: *Every building was at least half-demolished and most of them were total wrecks. In Berlin, ruined structures were abandoned but in Dusseldorf so much had been decimated—93 percent of the houses were uninhabitable— that bombed-out places had to be used. You looked at a house. It seemed to be a complete ruin. But when you looked closer you saw that above the two lower stories, which were burned out with only the upright girders remaining, a fresh brick wall had been built and crude windows put in, and behind them was a light. Next to this solitary eyrie the family wash hung in a space open to the elements.*

At war's end an estimated thirty to sixty million Europeans had become displaced persons. (By contrast, the figure at the end of the First World War was six million.) This resulted in massive migrations, five years of continental crisscrossing involving repatriates, expellees, fugitives, prisoners of war, forced laborers, and concentration camp survivors—including people from every conceivable European background.

An American journalist accompanying concentration camp survivors from Germany to Palestine reported: *At every station we saw other trains loaded with other refugees. In ancient third-class carriages like ours we saw Poles going East, and in battered freight cars Volksdeutsche going West. Sometimes our trains and the trains carry-*

President Harry Truman plays the piano as actress Lauren Bacall listens and poses. The year was 1945.

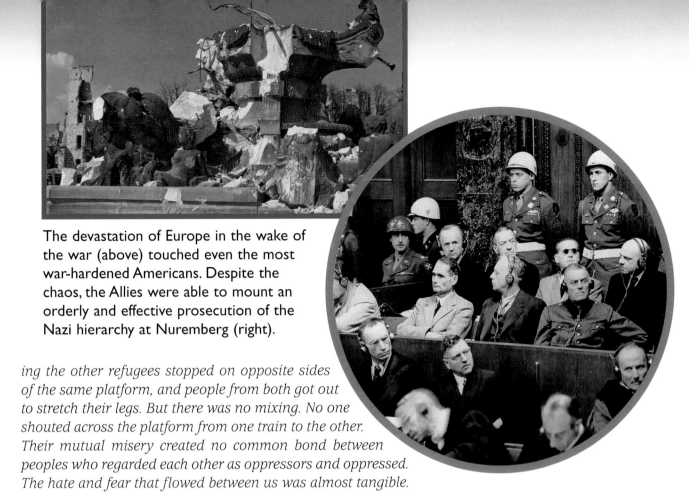

The devastation of Europe in the wake of the war (above) touched even the most war-hardened Americans. Despite the chaos, the Allies were able to mount an orderly and effective prosecution of the Nazi hierarchy at Nuremberg (right).

ing the other refugees stopped on opposite sides of the same platform, and people from both got out to stretch their legs. But there was no mixing. No one shouted across the platform from one train to the other. Their mutual misery created no common bond between peoples who regarded each other as oppressors and oppressed. The hate and fear that flowed between us was almost tangible.

For many Americans, the conditions in Europe served as a reminder that the postwar world was likely to be a hard and ominous place.

America Finds a Middle Class

War prosperity had created a new middle class in the United States. America was about to go on a nationwide spending spree. Gas rationing ended on August 15, 1945, and for a short time long lines became a common sight at gas stations as people filled up their tanks for the first time since Pearl Harbor. In Joliet, Illinois, a group of townspeople planned a gas-rationing-card funeral. Coupons were thrown into an open casket in front of the city hall. *Newsweek* reported that an undertaker had promised a caisson and two black horses to carry the casket through the streets to the site selected for the big bonfire. But Joliet's mayor decided to call it off when the local OPA objected.

It took more than a full year for the long awaited boom in automobile production to materialize. One observer noted: *The year's second coal strike was estimated to have cost the motor industry upward of 100,000 cars, while the earlier strikes in steel and coal resulted in an estimated loss of 1,200,000 passenger cars.*

Throughout 1946, assembly lines slowed down, and in some cases stopped completely due to strikes and shortages. Necessary items in short supply ranged from glass, bearings, and fuel pumps in January to cushion springs, clutches, and crankshafts in June, to copper and castings in December, along with many other much-sought-after items. The demand for all goods exceeded the supply. A 1946 Toastmaster ad

The devastation caused by the atom bomb (left, Hiroshima's city hall after the blast) stunned even the scientists who had tested the device in New Mexico. Yet it paled in comparison with bombs in existence only a few years later.

("This treasured gift of fortunate brides is new in beauty and performance...but old in experience"), after promising "years of blissful breakfasts," added: "If your dealer hasn't got it now, he'll gladly take your order—and do his best to deliver. Our production is steadily mounting, but the demand is still far ahead of us."

Finally, in 1947, the boom began in earnest. That year, J. Gordon Lippincott, in his book, *Design for Business*, wrote: "If hard-headed businessmen could build up...the cosmetic industry in a few years, and do it on sheer emotional appeal to the American woman, there is no reason why common everyday objects such as alarm clocks, prefabricated homes, hair curlers, and helicopters should not be sold on the same basis." Lippincott claimed the range of the American designer's vision should encompass everything "from lipsticks to locomotives."

The boom at the end of the 1940s did encompass a wide range of items that were totally new. It included everything from Henry Dreyfuss's classic Model 500 telephone to automatic pin-spotters, which spelled the end of employment as pin boys for quite a few (necessarily agile) youths, to "flex-o-matic" padding on dashboards; from sleekly curvaceous and brightly colored electric typewriters to reclining chairs; from radio-phonograph consoles to frozen fish; from automatic washers ("Breakfast with the family while the clothes wash super clean") to modernistic collages in advertising. In 1948 General Motors sold a million Frigidaire refrigerators.

That same year Cadillac became the first car with tail fins. (Designer Harley Earl said he got the idea from the P-38 fighter plane.) Pan Am was showing movies in the air, offering "sleeperette" service, and their new Boeing 70-ton double-decker clippers featured a cocktail lounge. More families were flying. One advertising photo included a baby (with stuffed animal) asleep in his crib. Tied around the crib was an oversized identification tag which read: "I am Jackie Hall. I am traveling alone. My grandmother is Mrs. O. J. Villere who is meeting me at LaGuardia Airfield." Another ad with a similar photo featured a Pan American Baby Kit, informing you that "stewardesses are instructed to relieve the mother in mixing formulas whenever possible."

By the spring of 1947 the purchasing power of the average American family was more than 30 percent higher than it had been in 1939. For the first time millions of families could afford vacation trips. In 1948 New York had become the first state in which residents' combined estimated spending on travel surpassed $1 billion. In the summer of

1949, a drive-in restaurant in Los Angeles installed the first "motormat," which the manufacturer described as, "a wheel-like layout that has 20 parking stalls, each served by an electronically controlled food carriage. The motorist checks off his order, puts it in the carriage with enough money, presses a button, and the carriage moves off to the kitchen. There an attendant fills the order, makes change, and sends the carriage back to the car. The motormat operates 16 hours a day and can serve 960 cars in that period."

Although many women returned to full-time domesticity, many others continued to hold down jobs. There were fewer women working in 1948 than in 1944 but more than before Pearl Harbor. *Charm,* the first magazine devoted exclusively to women who work, grew in popularity, especially in urban areas. Though it was too far ahead of its time to rival the success of more traditional women's magazines, *Charm* was the first publication to alert advertisers to the enormous purchasing power of working women.

In their press kit, the salespeople at *Charm* tried to lure advertisers with the new purchasing power of the American woman:

Who goes through more girdles? Women who work and dress from the skin out daily! Their hat-to-heel wardrobe warrants buying girdles in pairs, slips in several lengths, bras in varied shapes. Multiple-purchase customers, they consider good lingerie the natural foundation for the good clothes they wear from Monday to Sunday. They don't wait for an occasion to put on a girdle—they "go out" every day. They don't need a trousseau to justify a chest filled with lingerie—they dress up every day. Women who work put over $5 billion on their backs and they're putting the ready-to-wear business on its feet.

The magazine was short-lived, but manufacturers started producing more women's undergarments than ever before.

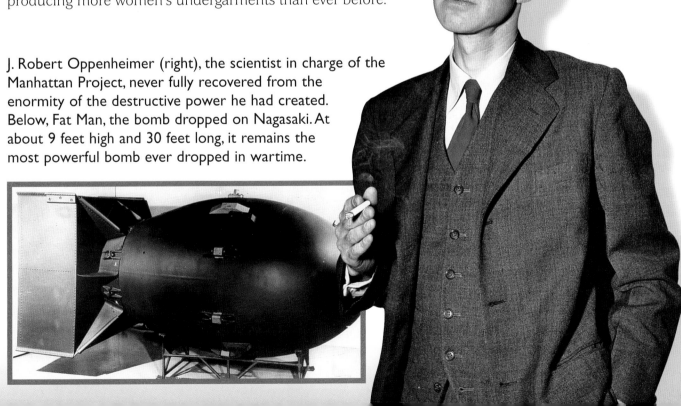

J. Robert Oppenheimer (right), the scientist in charge of the Manhattan Project, never fully recovered from the enormity of the destructive power he had created. Below, Fat Man, the bomb dropped on Nagasaki. At about 9 feet high and 30 feet long, it remains the most powerful bomb ever dropped in wartime.

And Then There Was Television...

At the start of 1945, there were 9 television stations operating in the entire nation. Of these, WRGB in Schenectady, New York, was on the air the longest—nine hours a week. WABD in Manhattan was second with seven and a half hours and WXYZ (Paramount Studio's live-talent programs) in Hollywood was third with six hours per week.

But as a 1945 DuMont ("Precision electronics and television") ad stated: *Teleflash: More than 90 requests for permission to construct and operate commercial television stations are on file with the Federal Communications Commission. As only a few channels are available for television, the number of stations in a trading area is limited. In consequence, options are already being sought for desirable "air time." More than 60 advertising agencies have installed television departments.*

At the same time, Philco ("Famous for quality the world over") announced the first network: *Chain television is here! With the recent dedication of the new Philco relay transmitter at Mt. Rose, New Jersey, the first television network, linking Philadelphia, New York and Schenectady, is in actual operation today. Now Philadelphians enjoy clear reception of programs from New York through their local Philco television stations. Thus the first step has been taken through which millions will eventually witness events that take place thousands of miles away.*

Some 7,000 sets were sold in 1946. In the summer of 1948, newspapers started showing pictures of new "television trucks": *Giant mobile units, making possible sight-and-sound broadcasts of news, sporting events and other features from locations remote from the television station's transmitting point.*

Later that year, Milton Berle hosted the first telethon, working 24 hours straight (subsisting on sandwiches and coffee) and raising over $100,000 for the Damon Runyon Cancer Fund. In 1948, 172,000 television sets were sold in the United States. The figure for the year 1950: 5 million.

In the years after the war, the issue of communism was debated in the streets of America (above) as anti-Soviet protesters picketed leftist rallies in venues like Carnegie Hall (above, left).

A New Age Called Atomic

Initially, almost all Americans responded with awe to the dropping of the atomic bomb upon the Japanese cities of Hiroshima and Nagasaki. The blasts were followed by a seemingly unending series of newspaper and magazine articles, radio programs, and public lectures with titles like, "Atomic Bomb: Salvation or Doom?" and "Has mankind gone too far?"

But soon Americans began doing what they usually do when faced with something new and unique: they absorbed it into the popular culture. By Christmas 1945 several bomb-related songs had appeared. Karl Davis and Harty Taylor released "When the Atom Bomb Fell" and Slim Gailord recorded "Atomic Cocktail." Others soon followed: "Atomic Power," "Atomic Boogie," "Atom and Evil"—even the "Atomic Polka." Benny Binion's Las Vegas gambling house, the Horseshoe Club (with its famous wall of genuine $10,000 bills), was the first to feature a mushroom cloud picture postcard. There were atomic socks (embroidered with mushroom clouds), atomic shakes, atomic trucking, atomic rug-cleaning, atomic bicycle repair, atomic exterminators.

World War II had its own vocabulary, from *ack-ack* (antiaircraft fire) to *zero* (a Japanese fighter plane). Even seldom-used *Q* contributed *Quisling* and *Quonset hut*. So also did the new atomic age. The average American was suddenly hearing about plutonium, uranium, thorium, dosimeters, and detonation waves. But while the words and phrases of the war were part of a vocabulary of victory, the language of the atomic age brought only apprehension and unease.

On March 5, 1946, when Winston Churchill made his famous Iron Curtain speech, the Cold War was already underway and communism was on the march in Europe. In February 1948 Czechoslovakia fell to the Communists, and in June the Soviets blockaded Berlin. The North Atlantic Treaty Organization (NATO) was formed in April 1949, and the Berlin Airlift broke the blockade in May, raising American spirits. But the good feeling didn't last long. On August 29, 1949, the Soviets exploded their first atomic bomb. Now there were two superpowers. China fell to the Communists. When, on December 16, Mao arrived in Moscow to conclude an alliance with Stalin, President Truman had already authorized the development of the hydrogen bomb.

The 1940s ended with much of the nation feeling weary, uncertain, fearful. For many Americans, nuclear war seemed a very real possibility. The comfortable optimism of the New York World's Fair just a decade earlier was replaced with apprehension. It dawned on people that change—even progress—might not be such a good thing; technology could create a future one might want no part of. The planned "cities of the future" were now obsolete, and some wondered if there would even be a tomorrow in which to build them. A respite from all the turmoil, a break in the action, was sorely needed. For all the creative and material energy released during the course of the decade, America frequently hoped the next 10 years would be quieter—much, much quieter.

HOMECOMING

n August 1945 a baker in Pittsburgh placed a small hand-lettered sign in his front window that said, simply: "Welcome Home." Later that day he found that someone had added, "Two best words in the English language."

A woman from Vermont wrote:

It was just the sweetest time. The end of summer, from right before V-J day when we knew it was just a matter of days, hours maybe, to the first frost was like a magical period of grace. I remember one day I was taking my Uncle Ed—he must've been near 80 then—to visit Patricia and the kids. He loved the old brick railroad depot at Lyndonville, so I would always swing by there. And when we got to the station there were about 35 or 40 boys, on their way home from the separation center at Camp Edwards, getting off the train. Some of the soldiers still on the train were leaning out the windows, saying goodbye or just smiling quietly. About a dozen people, mostly small children, were watching. And I remember Uncle Ed said to me, "They're so young," and his eyes filled with tears. I don't know if it was for these boys who were finally safe or for the ones that had been killed. Probably a little of both.

A Navy lieutenant returning from the Pacific, recalled: *I was on the train from Chicago to New York. Last leg. I already felt like I was home. Kwajalein and Eniwetok were already a hundred years ago. When we got to Pittsburgh it was the middle of the night. We had maybe fifteen or twenty minutes, so I stirred*

myself. I'd been at the same station when I left to enlist. I was working for the Bessemer and Lake Erie Railroad. Living in Greenville, and when I got my orders, I'd taken the train first to Pittsburgh, then to Philadelphia, finally to New York. So I got off the train and just walked around the platform for a few minutes. Of course I was thinking back to over two years earlier. And as I stood there I felt an incredible ease. A lightness, a sweet physical relief that for some reason I hadn't felt before. It was as if my whole body was saying to the fates (that somehow inhabit the middle of the night air of the Pittsburgh train station), "Thanks."

And a fighter pilot, also back from the Pacific, remembers reuniting with his wife: *One day I got off the train at Grand Central. Barb was there and she looked great. We went off and had breakfast together. And as far as I was concerned, that was the end of my war.*

Opposite, the 442nd Regimental Combat Team and, left, the 86th Division arrive home to tumultuous welcomes. A Broadway parade (left, center) welcomes Allied commander in chief Gen. Dwight D. Eisenhower (seated in uniform in the front car).

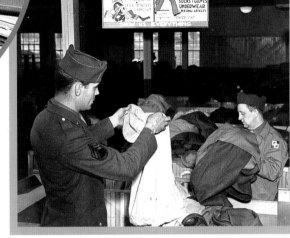

Below, the first veterans to receive their honorable discharges after V-E Day leave Fort Dix, New Jersey, for home, May 12, 1946. Officially, the only military gear a soldier was allowed to take home with him (above) was his uniform. In the postwar rush, soldiers often brought back other gear as well.

BUY VICTORY BONDS

This Norman Rockwell painting (above, left), used during the war to promote the sale of War Bonds, graced the cover of *The Saturday Evening Post* on May 26, 1945, shortly after V-E Day. Many soldiers, like John Culhane, above, right, returned home to greet children they barely knew. Below, they danced the conga in Lafayette Park opposite the White House on August 14, 1945, as they waited for official word that the war was over.

Happy and thankful veterans of the fighting in the European Theater of Operations crowd the decks as their troopship docks in New York on June 17, 1945; they are part of the first division to return from overseas. Some husbands and wives didn't have to wait to reach America to be reunited. The couple at left, for example, from Davenport, Iowa—he in the signal corps, she a nurse—are reunited at an army evacuation hospital in France.

LIFE AFTER THE WAR

Two of the most popular movies right after the war were Frank Capra's *It's a Wonderful Life* and William Wyler's *The Best Years of Our Lives*, both released in 1946. Capra's sentimental story about a man and his guardian angel was full of nostalgia for American small-town life, reflecting the yearning of many people for a time and place before the war that was much less complicated. (No atomic age angst in Bedford Falls.) The movie was vintage Capra: a populist fantasy of an idealized American communal coziness.

Conversely, *The Best Years of Our Lives* was about three returning veterans readjusting to civilian life; it was powerful, poignant, and emblematic of the adjustments needed in the postwar years. One of its stars was Harold Russell, a double amputee who was not a professional actor. Wyler's previous work included *Mrs. Miniver*, a movie some credit with swaying American opinion toward England. One of the greatest movies ever made, *The Best Years of Our Lives* summed up the plight of returning servicemen with the memorable line: "Last year it was kill Japs. This year it's make money."

To help the returning veteran, the government enacted the GI Bill of Rights, a landmark piece of legislation that made it possible for thousands of former servicemen to fashion better lives for themselves and their families by granting loans and providing education. It greatly benefited all of America, for it virtually assured the creation of an educated and productive middle class.

For many returning veterans the path to civilian success involved three steps: Go to college on the GI Bill; get a good job; buy a nice house (with a GI loan). The home was often their first, and it was usually in one of the new suburban developments springing up by the hundreds across the country.

When asked if the uniformity of the houses in Levittown bothered him, an original resident said: "I didn't care, not at all. The first time my Uncle Alex came out to visit he said two things: There's no trees and all the houses look the same. I told him trees will grow, and after fighting the Nazis at Monte Cassino, there's no way I'm going back to share a cramped bedroom in Brooklyn with two brothers."

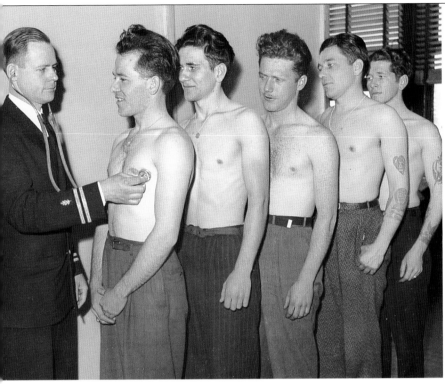

Left, the Sullivan brothers, of Waterloo, Iowa, ranging in age from 19 to 27, enlisted when one of their friends, William Ball, was killed at Pearl Harbor. All five brothers were killed when their ship, the USS *Juneau*, was sunk near Guadalcanal on November 12, 1942. The five brothers were immortalized in the 1944 film, *The Fighting Sullivans*, which remained popular even after the war was over.

Left, Jimmy Stewart as George Bailey trying to get Uncle Billy to remember—a defining scene in *It's a Wonderful Life*. Only a mild success in the '40s, this picture has become a Christmastime TV staple in the decades since. Below, in *The Best Years of Our Lives,* Fred Derry (played by Dana Andrews, center) meets Homer Parrish, a handless veteran (played by Harold Russell, left), as they wait for a plane to take them home at the end of the war. Russell, a double amputee, won the 1946 Academy Award for Best Supporting Actor. *Best Years* was his only film.

Above, Audie Murphy, the most decorated American soldier of World War II, receives the Légion d'Honneur from France's Gen. Charles de Gaulle. The Texas native went on to have a brief film career, capped by *To Hell and Back* in 1955.

The V-J issue of *Yank*, the army weekly, displayed the latest civilian fashions to soldiers about to leave military life. ("This is a suit..." the article wryly began.) Former servicemen found jobs and housing scarce at first, and some employers were ready to take advantage of the "buyers' market" by offering low wages. This often resulted in protest marches like the one below near the state capitol in Harrisburg, Pennsylvania. Bottom, the family of a former navy cook sleeps on the lawn of the Los Angeles city hall in protest of the lack of housing.

Some returning servicemen felt right at home in Quonset-hut housing provided them on many university campuses. Right, the family of a former marine lieutenant moves into just such a home on the Evanston, Illinois, campus of Northwestern University.

Women veterans also used their GI Bill eligibility mortgages and business-loan guarantees, as well as for their education. The women below, right, attend a Spanish class at the University of California under the GI Bill.

With the return of soldiers from the war, the inevitable increase in the birth-rate took place, giving rise to the baby boomer generation. Above, one family in Troy, New York, had seven children before the war, and then seven more after the war. New sub-urban developments, like Levit-town, New York (right and below), had wide open spaces in which children could play. Suburbia soon developed a toddler-based economy.

Mary Jane Inge

Mary Jane Inge was born in Mobile, Alabama, and spent her whole life there. She watched America change from the porch of her comfortable Southern home.

War rationing affected each group and individual differently, but it almost always left an indelible mark.

My father was head of the Gas Rationing Board and no daughter of his was going to ride around in a car that was not used for anything except getting back and forth to work.

The thing I remember most is—because I had the big feet—shoe rationing. You take shoes away from a teenage girl and you have got trouble on your hands. Three pairs a year! You had a pair to go to school in, a pair to go to church and Sunday school in, and if you were lucky, a winter pair...Forget the meat, forget the sugar, forget the gas, it was the shoes, because I...and I think I've had a thing about shoes ever since.

After the war, life in Mobile returned to normal. Veterans had the opportunity to attend college and think about their future.

The boys, actually when they came home from the service, had money for some reason. They all had these life insurance policies, and some of them took that in cash. They were all able to go to college—people that had...would never have been able to go

to college—on the GI Bill. And they were given an allowance for living expenses.

So the fun part about it is, as we all laughed and said, there were five men for every girl. There was no such thing as not being able to get a date. And in Mobile, the social life started back, the Mardi Gras ball started back. And the parties started back, and we had a wonderful time. When we first met, thirteen people got married between September and December, of my friends—thirteen!

After so many marriages, the married couples wanted to start having children and the baby boom was under way.

We lived all together and all of us had children about the same time. In fact, this was the beginning of the baby boom. My oldest son was born on the 25th of January at 6:30 in the morning and he was the 25th baby born in the Mobile infirmary since midnight...In a small town—and that was just one of three hospitals.

And all the new mothers, we all sat out in the yard—there was no air conditioning—and we nursed in the yard and we sewed in the afternoons. When the children got up from their nap, we'd sit outside with playpens or baby buggies or strollers and sit...bring our own chairs and sit and visit all afternoon. There must have been three hundred of us with our babies.

"DEWEY DEFEATS TRUMAN"

A Miami woman remembers election night, 1948: *My oldest brother, Tim, was a sophomore at Northwestern and worked in a student organization for Harry Truman. Of course we'd seen the polls and we'd heard H. V. Kaltenborn on the radio say that Truman did not have the necessary votes to win. It was Tim who called from school and told us Truman had won. And, being in Chicago, he'd picked up about a dozen copies of the famous "Dewey Defeats Truman" newspaper.*

I remember him telling us that there were 3 or 4 different editions, all printed with that same banner headline. He took one of the front pages and put it up on his dormitory wall. It was, along with his Johnny Mize baseball and his 8x10 glossy of Alexis Smith, his most prized possession.

The overconfident Dewey was not the only person to have his hopes dashed in the Forties. The eccentric, enigmatic (but not yet reclusive) billionaire Howard Hughes, referred to by the press as the "World's Richest Man," managed to build the world's largest airplane, a flying boat dubbed the *Spruce Goose*, only to have the craft consigned to its hangar after one short demonstration flight. Another flamboyant entrepreneur, Preston Tucker, introduced his version of the car of the future, only to have it fail amid accusations of fraud and countercharges that Detroit's automakers had done him in.

Harry Truman not only won the 1948 election, he won praise from most Americans for settling strikes at home and for such foreign policy successes as the Truman Doctrine and the Marshall Plan.

Truman took his campaign to the people (right, at a whistle stop in Indiana), while Dewey (inset, far right) stayed in the cities. The photo at right of Dewey and running mate Earl Warren in a cow pasture with pressed shirts and polished dress shoes backfired badly.

Other winners of the postwar Forties included Citation, racing's Triple Crown winner, and the game of baseball, which enjoyed renewed pop-ularity.

The 1947 World Series between the Yankees and the Dodgers was a classic seven-game encounter that reminded many people just how thrilling the national pastime could be. The Series' inspired play included some notable firsts: first pinch-hit home run (Yogi Berra); first time a player scored eight runs in seven games (Yankee Billy Johnson); first time a player hit three triples (also Billy Johnson).

It was also the first time a black man played in the World Series (Jackie Robinson). And it was the first World Series to be shown on television. Across America, people actually got to see lefty Joe Page jump over the bullpen fence as he came to pitch. They got to see Spec Shea, Phil Rizutto, and Pee Wee Reese.

They watched Cookie Lavagetto break up Bill Bevens' no-hitter with two outs in the ninth (and in the process win the game for Brooklyn.) And the fans watching on television witnessed one of the greatest catches in baseball history when Al Gianfriddo robbed Joe DiMaggio of a 415-foot three-run home run. Fans everywhere agreed: New York City was the right place for the first televised World Series.

The *Spruce Goose*, built for the serious purpose of providing transportation for military hardware and troops, was introduced too late to do its job. Builder Howard Hughes flew the plane just once.

Opposite, below, Preston Tucker drives his dream car in January 1950, just days after being acquitted of fraud charges. Only 50 Tuckers were ever manufactured. Above, Citation is so far ahead of the field in the 1948 Pimlico Stakes that there do not seem to be any other horses in the race. There weren't any; no other horses were entered against the legendary Thoroughbred. (Owner Warren Wright donated the purse to the Damon Runyon Cancer Fund.)

Baseball held the nation's attention with the 1947 Subway Series between the Yankees and the Dodgers. At left, a vendor sells an official program listing the years when the Yankees had won championships. Fans filled the seats four hours before the first pitch. The games were broadcast worldwide for the first time, including to Moscow. (The Yanks won, four games to three.)

Above, President Truman addresses the last session of UNCIO (the United Nations Conference on International Organizations) in San Francisco in June of 1948. The conference laid a solid foundation for the UN, which would later take up quarters in New York City. One of the early issues dealt with by the United Nations was the partition of Palestine into independent Jewish and Arab states. The formation of the state of Israel was celebrated in many US cities: at right, Abba Eban and Moshe Sharet, Israeli diplomats, flank the flag of Israel in May 1949. Below, a Camden, New Jersey, rally celebrates Israeli independence that same month.

Bill DeFossett

From the moment he first saw the men of the 369th Infantry Regiment, the Harlem Hellfighters, marching down New York's Fifth Avenue, Bill DeFossett knew he wanted to be one of them. After fighting on Saipan, he returned to Harlem, married, joined the New York City Police Department, and lived in the same building as Bill "Bojangles" Robinson and Paul Robeson.

DeFossett was guided by his parents and the example of Jackie Robinson in dealing with racism.

Well...my father was colored, I was a Negro, my son is black, and my grandson is African-American. So you know you take your pick...It's like your indoctrination; you're taught certain things at an early age. In other words, your parents have to focus you in the right direction, they have to tell you: If you're going for a job, you have to be twice as capable as a white person to get that job. And if you don't get it, don't come home with your head in your hand. Just hold your head up and start out again.

It's the same as they talk about Jackie Robinson. It's a terrible thing to be out there playing baseball and a guy spit in your face and you can't do anything about it...And that's the thing that Jackie Robinson should be credited for—keeping his temper. Not for hitting home runs and stealing bases and all that stuff, because white people do that. But he had to endure so much, you know. The team checks into the hotel and everybody gets a room but him, and he's got to scrounge around in the black neighborhood to find somebody that'll let him stay the night.

During the war, DeFossett found that prejudice momentarily disappeared in the heat of battle.

We all got along well during the invasion. And we had no particular problems. There's one thing about combat, or crisis situations. When you're all caught up together in the same boat, you don't have a chance to express your prejudices. If you and I are about to get shot or maybe drowned off a sinking ship, if you hold out your hand and I grab it, you're not going to say, well, I'm going to reach only for white hands, or I'm going to reach only for black hands, or whatnot; you reach out for any hands that'll save you. It's only during nice times that you can exercise your prejudice.

Coming home from the war, DeFossett was on a troop train that was filled with many war brides en route to their new homes.

Well, it was quite an enjoyable trip because we were in the minority and the women were anxious to find out about the United States....We were dropping off brides at the various locations— some were pleased and some were not pleased. Sometimes we got to a station and it wasn't even a station; it was just a place where the train stopped and you got off. And the bride would want to know. Is this the place my husband told me about, where he was the big shot in town?

A LIVING PORTRAIT

Postwar revelations of Communist spy activities shocked and outraged Americans. They were angry and fearful to discover that within the nation existed a clandestine netherworld of highly organized and extremely efficient cells of agents bent on the destruction (or domination) of the United States by the Soviet Union. The country's psyche was deeply wounded, and paranoia sometimes resulted.

Even children were affected. One recollection of the era: *Every year in late May, we would take the train from Milwaukee to Rhinelander to visit relatives. The whole trip took 8 hours. One of the very last stops (I think it was next-to-last) was a tiny place called Elcho. (By now it was getting close to midnight.) The station was invariably deserted. It was always foggy and cold. In May of 1949, after we'd made the trip, my young cousins Henry (who was six) and Margaret (who was four) started having terrible nightmares about how the Communists in the Elcho station would get them. They would wake up screaming and either Aunt Gerda, Aunt Edna, or my mother would have to go in and reassure them. My oldest brother, Bob, who was fifteen, thought it was a real hoot. He'd walk around making up tabloid headlines like, "Feds Nab Reds in Elcho," "Pinko Plot Hatched in Deserted Depot," or "Top Cop Seeks Microfilm in Moose Suit." Of course, it was totally ridiculous, but I'm sure little Henry and Margaret weren't the only children in America having very real nightmares about Communists coming to get them.*

The postwar era gave birth to its own movie genre. However, few of the films dealt with Communist espionage, *Pickup on South Street* being a notable exception. The protagonists were often ex-servicemen dealing with the war's harsh aftermath. In *Dead Reckoning,* Humphrey Bogart investigates the mysterious death of his old army buddy. In *Cornered,* Dick Powell is after the man who betrayed him in a prison camp during the war. These protagonists were not only war-weary, they were weary of appeals to their sense of patriotism. In *Ride the Pink Horse,* Robert Montgomery (who had in real life commanded a destroyer during the war) plays Lucky Gagin, a war hero who seeks revenge on a gangster. When the government agent who is also chasing the gangster appeals to Gagin's sense of duty, he replies: "Don't wave any flags at me, copper. I've seen too many flags."

Right, physicist Klaus Fuchs, the German Communist who passed atomic secrets to the Soviets. Opposite, left, Alger Hiss examines a photo of his accuser, Whitaker Chambers, at a HUAC session.

Left, Hollywood actors (from left) Robert Montgomery, George Murphy, and Ronald Reagan wave after testifying before the House Un-American Activities Committee (HUAC), which investigated Communist activities in the US. Below, leading Republican members of HUAC meet at Chairman J. Parnell Thomas's New Jersey home in March 1948. Future president Richard Nixon, then a representative from California, is on the right.

Right, well-known Hollywood figures (including Humphrey Bogart, Lauren Bacall, Gene Kelly, Danny Kaye, and June Havoc) fly to Washington to confront HUAC.

President Truman relied very heavily on James V. Forrestal, the first secretary of defense in charge of the unified armed forces. Forrestal's resignation in 1949, his hospitalization for nervous exhaustion, and his eventual suicide, came as a blow to Truman and contributed to his decision not to seek a another term in 1952.

The Berlin Airlift of 1948-49, below, was a crowning achievement in the early days of the Cold War. It demonstrated American resolve not to be intimidated by the Soviet Union. At right, Truman awards the Distinguished Service Medal to Maj. Gen. William "Wild Bill" Donovan for creating and operating the Office of Strategic Services (OSS), an American intelligence agency of World War II. Uncomfortable with cloak-and-dagger operations, Truman was to eliminate the OSS.

Above, George C. Marshall (center), a great general in wartime, became the genius behind the restoration of Europe. While Mao Tse-tung's new Communist government in China met with the West (below, left), the question "Who lost China?" became important in the 1952 election. Below, right, J. Edgar Hoover, director of the FBI, shown addressing an American Legion convention in Boston in 1949, would remain preoccupied with investigating subversion for decades.

America was facing difficult issues at home as well. Although Jackie Robinson (shown at left in a run-down) broke the color barrier in baseball, real progress in civil rights was slow in coming. Above, a black student who was admitted by the University of Oklahoma only after the school was ordered to do so by the Supreme Court in 1948, sits in a segregated anteroom and not in the classroom.

Two leaders of the black community, Rev. Adam Clayton Powell Jr. (top), first elected to Congress in 1944, and Ralph J. Bunche, undersecretary of the United Nations (center), board a plane bound for Ghana with Richard L. Jones, U.S. ambassador to Liberia.

Below, a still from Elia Kazan's 1947 film *Gentleman's Agreement*, based on Laura Z. Hobson's novel, about a magazine writer (Gregory Peck, left) exposing anti-Semitism in high society by masquerading as a Jew. The film won the Academy Award for Best Picture.

Women's issues were beginning to get serious attention in American society. Spencer Tracy had to deal with Katharine Hepburn as a workplace equal in George Cukor's 1949 movie, *Adam's Rib, left*. Below, a protest by mothers for more day care in 1946.

BRAVE NEW WORLDS

The postwar economic boom was also an era of rapid and far-reaching technological advances. Americans found that their language was sprouting a whole bunch of new words and abbreviations: cybernetics, early-warning radar, intercontinental ballistic missile, UNIVAC, UFO, and DDT. There was a heightened interest in anything related to outer space. Chuck Yaeger's breaking of the sound barrier captured the imagination of many Americans, as did the alleged crash of a UFO outside Roswell, New Mexico. Many people started to believe in flying saucers. Sales of telescopes soared as amateur astronomers watched the night skies for evidence of interplanetary life.

At the same time, the atomic age came to the classroom. Tests asked students in science class to identify monazite, thorium, cadmium rods, and fissionable isotopes. Schoolchildren too young to read about the critical mass for plutonium could content themselves with a widespread array of toy jet planes and flying saucers while munching candies with names like Jet Propellium and Atomic Firecrackers.

The advertising business really blossomed in the late Forties. Most Americans were eager to buy luxury items, and advertising became increasingly sophisticated. A veteran who grew up in St. Louis and was wounded at Anzio recalled how many people felt at the time:

You've got to remember that from the stock market crash in September '29 to V-J Day in August '45—that's sixteen years—and, except for the end of '40 and all of '41, it's either Depression or war. So it's no surprise that after the war ended most people wanted something new in their pleasure. I know I did.

The television industry was still in its infancy, but it was growing very rapidly. When advertising and television met, the consumer culture was born. Electric guitars were starting to be heard. Aaron "T-Bone" Walker (the "T-Bone" derived from his middle name: Thibeaux) came up with a new sound, a style that lent the blues a stinging, late-night-jazz feel, which single-handedly forged the modern urban blues sound. Many of the youngsters who heard his records ran out and bought electric guitars. One of them was B. B. King, the Memphis blues guitarist who later came to be regarded as a founder of rock-and-roll.

Above, the modern kitchen, circa 1948, a gold mine for Madison Avenue advertising in postwar America. "Serious" conceptions of flying saucers peppered the newspapers (top, left) like this notion proposed by Alex Tremulus. The success of Edwin Land's instant photography (below) in 1947 made every claim put forth by technology seem possible.

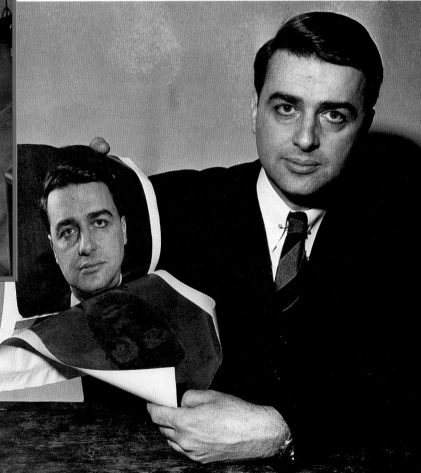

The US atomic bomb tests conducted at Bikini Atoll in the Pacific, left, inspired both full-body radiation suits, above, and, paradoxically, the scantiest of swimwear.

The late Forties saw a new era of exploration on a variety of frontiers. On October 14, 1947, Capt. Charles E. "Chuck" Yeager in the Bell *X-1* rocket plane (top) became the first man to break through the sound barrier. Above, John W. Mauchly and J. Presper Eckert were expanding the reach of the computer by developing ENIAC in a basement laboratory at the University of Pennsylvania.

Prof. Eliezer Sukenik of Hebrew University (right) began to unroll and unravel the archeological find of the decade, the Dead Sea Scrolls, containing 2,000-year-old commentaries, pieces of the Scriptures, and other religious texts.

Above, new chemicals (such as DDT, originally a defense against typhus-carrying lice), were being developed during the Forties as part of the ongoing fight against disease-spreading pests. Below, Norwegian ethnologist Thor Heyerdahl sailed his *Kon-Tiki* across the ocean to prove the feat was possible in ancient times.

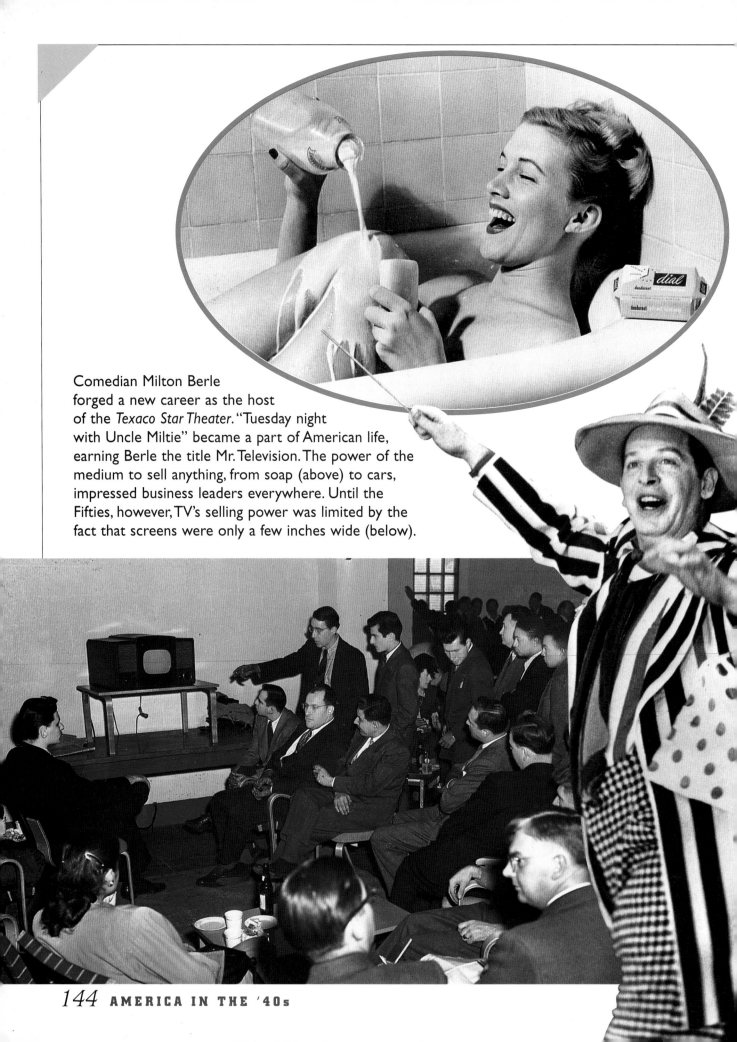

Comedian Milton Berle
forged a new career as the host
of the *Texaco Star Theater*. "Tuesday night
with Uncle Miltie" became a part of American life,
earning Berle the title Mr. Television. The power of the
medium to sell anything, from soap (above) to cars,
impressed business leaders everywhere. Until the
Fifties, however, TV's selling power was limited by the
fact that screens were only a few inches wide (below).

The glazed look on the faces of children watching television—below, dressed as and watching Hopalong Cassidy—would become all too familiar to decades of American parents. Above, one of the biggest stars of early television was a wooden puppet named Howdy Doody, in a show presided over by Buffalo Bob Smith and Clarabel the Clown; it premiered in 1947. (The puppet strings were only slightly less visible on the early TV sets.)

MODERN TIMES

The postwar era wrought enormous changes in the arts. Abstract Expressionism dominated painting. It inherited the abstract from Kandinsky and the expressionism from Van Gogh, and added the saturated color field painting of Matisse. Sometimes called action painting, it featured bold strokes and visceral risk-taking. Its leading practitioners (Jackson Pollock, Willem de Kooning, Mark Rothko, Franz Kline, and Robert Motherwell) all seemed to combine a sensuous love of paint itself—its textures as well as its colors—with a life-on-the-edge attitude that made that school of painting a triumph and its home, New York City, the new capital of the international art world.

At the same time, bebop was revolutionizing jazz. Of Charlie Parker, its brilliantly innovative driving force, one critic wrote: "He brought a harder edge to the music, an emotional force and passion that held his supertechnical dexterity in subordination. His sound on alto is unforgettable." Bebop's complex harmonies and often oblique relationship to the beat powerfully reflected the postwar mood of a restless America.

Even classical music found exuberant expression, as maestros became celebrities known to the ordinary person. This was in no small part due to the advent of the long-playing record, the LP, which made listening to recorded music closer to a concert experience and permitted uninterrupted performances of longer symphonic pieces.

This new urban muscularity and postwar paranoia intersected in film noir. The genre brimmed with fear of the enemy within, of people who are not what they appear to be. The protagonist moves in a world of sinister shadows, odd camera angles, nightmares, and rain-soaked city streets at 2 AM. He is threatened by human grotesques and tempted by femmes fatales. He doesn't know whom to trust and no one is going to help him. He learns that he must rely solely on himself.

Although it would still be some time before America produced conductors on its own soil, European-trained meastros developed great orchestras in the late Forties that furthered public interest in and appreciation of classical music. Eugene Ormandy (above) developed the unique Philadelphia sound, while Ormandy's mentor, Arturo Toscanini (left) created the NBC Symphony, designing it specifically for radio and recorded performance.

Opposite, the influence of Christian Dior's New Look— the spirit of modernism translated into clothing— was felt throughout the fashion world. Right, a Dior gown is flanked by gowns by designers Lilly Daché (right) and Nettie Rosenstein.

Agnes De Mille, choreographer of such hit Broadway shows in the Forties as *Oklahoma!* (1943), *Carousel* (1945), and *Brigadoon* (1947), set the standard for a distinctively American art form: the musical. Below, she rehearses (left) for her celebrated 1945 ballet, *Rodeo*. Right, the dance sequences for *Brigadoon* were considered by many critics to be De Mille's masterpieces.

The Forties also saw new territory charted in the realm of serious theater. Marlon Brando and Jessica Tandy electrified the stage as Stanley Kowalski and Blanche DuBois in the 1947 Tennessee Williams hit, *A Streetcar Named Desire.* Their performances gave impetus to a new dramatic style known as Method acting.

It has been said that playwright Arthur Miller (left) elevated American theater to its pinnacle in the 1949 production of *Death of a Salesman*. Flouting every tenet of classical tragedy, Miller's story of the pathetic salesman, Willy Loman, whose greatest value in life is to be "well liked," has become a classic. Lee J. Cobb's portrayal of Loman (below, center) was a triumph that would be long remembered on Broadway.

The 1945 Hitchcock film, *Spellbound*, brought together three popular postwar themes: the mind, the macabre, and the menacing. Gregory Peck played an amnesiac who is helped by a psychiatrist, played by Ingrid Bergman (below). The dream sequences (right) were designed by Surrealist artist Salvador Dali.

Though they starred together in only four movies, Humphrey Bogart and Lauren Bacall (right) were emblematic of the couple of the Forties. He was tough but vulnerable, she clever and crackling with sexuality. The pair's devotion to one another was the stuff of Hollywood legend.

THE STORY OF A RECKLESS WOMAN!

Columbia Pictures
presents

RITA HAYWORTH · ORSON WELLES
in

The LADY *from* SHANGHAI

with
Everett SLOANE and Glenn ANDERS

Screenplay and Production by
Orson WELLES

Orson Welles again showed his mastery of storytelling on film with the 1948 film, *The Lady from Shanghai.* The final shoot-out scene in the room of mirrors has become a much-copied movie classic.

From Here to Eternity was released in 1953, but it owed much to the cinema of the Forties (and of course to James Jones's gritty novel). In the days before Pearl Harbor, Deborah Kerr and Burt Lancaster (right) play secret lovers, while Montgomery Clift and Frank Sinatra (below, center) are entertained in Rose's Cantina.

Below, Joltin' Joe DiMaggio, just two years away from retirement, speaks to fans on DiMaggio Day at Yankee Stadium in 1949. At left is Mel Allen, legendary voice of the Yankees.

In the late Forties, it became possible to get there in style, with, top right, Pan Am's giant Stratocruiser, and the luxury train, the *Twentieth Century Limited*, below. The train's dining lounge (right) was designed by Henry Dreyfuss.

As the Forties drew to a close, heavyweight champion Joe Louis visited singer Lena Horne while she was performing at the Mayfair Room in Chicago, fueling (unfounded) rumors of the couple's impending marriage.

On the eve of the Fifties, America was confronted with another crisis, this time on the Korean peninsula. Right, President Truman, addressing reservists, tried to prepare the nation for the prospect of having to fight overseas once again. At the decade's end, the tense atmosphere of international relations would be set for years to come.

Timescope

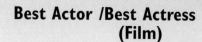

Shopping in 1949

Newspapers: Daily	$ .03
Sunday	$ .15
Woman's Jacket	$23.00
Dress	$17.00
Shoes	$9.00
Man's Suit	$105.00
Shoes	$15.00
Dinner at Schrafft's	$1.90
Round-Trip Airfare,	
New York to Paris	$407.00
Tickets to Broadway Play	$3.00
TV-radio-phonograph	
Console	$350.00
Cigar	$.10
Fifth Avenue (New York)	
6-room apartment	$19,000
Living Room Furniture Set,	$280.00

**Median Annual Income,
1949:** $2,992

The Envelope, Please...

Academy Award Winners
Best Picture / Best Director
(Film, if not Best Picture)

1940	Rebecca / John Ford (for The Grapes of Wrath)
1941	How Green Was My Valley / John Ford
1942	Mrs. Miniver / William Wyler
1943	Casablanca / Michael Curtiz
1944	Going My Way / Leo McCarey
1945	The Lost Weekend / Billy Wilder
1946	The Best Years of Our Lives / William Wyler
1947	Gentlemen's Agreement / Elia Kazan
1948	Hamlet / John Huston (for Treasure of Sierra Madre)
1949	All the King's Men / Joseph L. Mankiewicz (for A Letter to Three Wives)

Best Actor /Best Actress
(Film)

1940	James Stewart (The Philadelphia Story) Ginger Rogers (Kitty Foyle)
1941	Gary Cooper (Sergeant York) Joan Fontaine (Suspicion)
1942	James Cagney (Yankee Doodle Dandy) Greer Garson (Mrs. Miniver)
1943	Paul Lukas (Watch on the Rhine) Jennifer Jones (The Song of Bernadette)
1944	Bing Crosby (Going My Way) Ingrid Bergman (Gaslight)
1945	Ray Milland (The Lost Weekend) Joan Crawford (Mildred Pierce)
1946	Frederic March (The Best Years of Our Lives) Olivia DeHaviland (To Each His Own)
1947	Ronald Colman (A Double Life) Loretta Young (The Farmer's Daughter)
1948	Laurence Olivier (Hamlet) Jane Wyman (Johnny Belinda)
1949	Broderick Crawford (All the King's Men) Olivia DeHavilland (The Heiress)

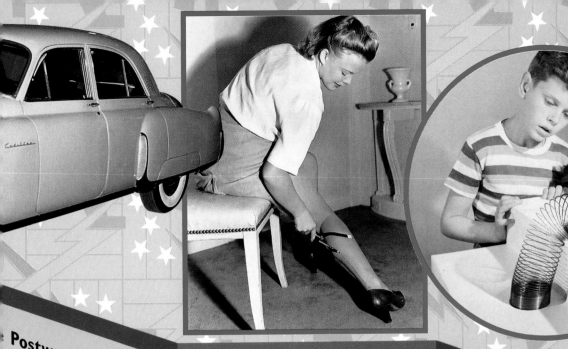

Postwar Auto Boom

Four Makes

	Average Price / Cars Sold:1947/1946
vrolet	$1,405 / 397,104/12,776
d	$1,528 / 372,917/34,439
mouth	$1,314 / 242, 524/none
dge	$1,486 / 156,126/420

xpensive Car of 1947: Cadillac
(Price:-$4,669 / 28,144 sold)

Passenger Cars Sold

—	181,000
0	2,787,456
5	**3,717,385**
0	**69,552**
)	**6,665,863**
s	6,674,796
s	8,002,259

Legacy of the Late '40s

Timex Watches	1946
Bikini Swimsuit	1946
Slinky (above, right)	1946
Ajax Cleanser	1947
L.P. Record	1948
Velcro	1948
Transistor	1948
Silly Putty	1949
Scrabble	1949
Prepared Cake Mixes	1949
Lego Building Blocks	1949

Fads of the Forties

Nylon Stockings	
"Kilroy Was Here"	1940
Lindy Hop	1941
Women's Convertible	1941
Day-to-Evening Suit	
Canasta	1944
Frozen Food	1946
"Howdy Doody	1948
for President" Buttons	
Cowboy and Indian Suits	1948
Erector Sets	1949
Roller Derby	1949
Lady Wrestlers	1949

Index

Page numbers in italics refer to illustrations.